Chinese Down-Under

Chinese people in Australia, their history here, and their influence, then and now.

By Patrick Grayson

Published by

Heart Space Publications
PO Box 1085
Daylesford
Victoria
3460
Australia
Tel +61 450260348
www.heartspacebooks.com
pat@heartspacebooks.com

Copyright © 2018 Pat Grayson

All rights reserved under international copyright conventions. No part of this book may be reproduced, stored in a retrieval system, or transmitted in any form or by any means electronic, mechanical, photocopying, recorded or otherwise without written permission from Heartspace Publications or Pat Grayson.

Whilst every care has been taken to check the accuracy of the information in this book, the publisher cannot be held responsible for any errors, omissions or originality.

Published in 2018 at Melbourne

ISBN 978-0-9944028-6-8

Testimonial

China Down Under is an insightful work addressing the ties between two interesting and culturally fascinating countries. It certainly addressed some topical issues, such as attitudes, commercial contributions and the tourism between the two. As someone who has never visited either countries, I really enjoyed the book as it was easy to read and informative. The headings instead of chapters worked really well and I also really liked the creative stories to break up the tone.

Maddy McGlynn (editor/proof reader; UK)

Introduction

I was chatting to publishing friends in China and they asked me if I had any books on China. 'What me? You are the Chinese people... I'm Australian, remember.' Then I asked, 'What sort of books are you looking for?' They replied, 'A book on Chinese people living in Australia and what their impressions are. After all, Australia and China are nearly neighbours, with just some sea between us.' 'Oh,' was all I said at the time, but the idea grew on me.

Of course, one must remember that the Chinese came to Australia long before any white people did, some say as early as the 1400s. They came to trade with the indigenous people of Australia and also sought minerals.

The first officially recorded Chinese immigrant that came to Australia in 1818 was called Mak Sai Ying, and, like many other Chinese immigrants, became a wealthy businessman. However, it is probable that there were many more here unofficially. Even now, China is Australia's largest trading partner, contributing to roughly thirty-two percent of the Australian trade (2017). The trade does not only come from China, as Australia offers China many products in return such as coal, iron ore, produce and technology. In 2017, China took seventy percent of Australia's wool. Australia also offers knowledge to China, like the collaboration between our two countries in the film industry, whereby China's massively growing film industry (which will soon be one of the largest in the world) has derived great benefit from the knowledge and support of Australian filmmakers.

Perhaps the biggest trade between our two countries is that of people. Last year, from Beijing alone, there were 1.6 million tourists who came to Australia. It goes both ways, as China was the second largest destination for Australian tourists, all going to see that marvelous country. Moreover, of the 500,000 international students who come to Australia to study each year, 10% are from China (with many ultimately becoming Australian citizens) and this figure is growing.

As a point of interest, international students (not only Chinese) studying in Australia, and the money they bring through living costs and education, accounts for Australia's third largest industry.

Of course, as the idea of this book took hold, I learnt all about Chinese-Australians and their contribution to this country. Below, you will learn of Chinese-Australians who fought in the great wars that Australia was involved in – many were heroes of great courage. There are interviews of Chinese-Australians or Chinese people who have lived here, who all shared their time and knowledge. The fascinating history of the early gold rush days is a given, as is Chinese involvement and contribution. Included are biographies of Chinese-Australians: a fashion designer, a dancer, a scientists, itinerate workers, a teacher, a heart transplant doctor, politicians and many who have had great success in their vocations. Nevertheless, not all are heroes or to be adulated, such as Sam Poo, a notorious bushranger of the early days, or the Chinese Triads who suck blood wherever they can.

This is an eclectic book, covering many topics and written with the Chinese reader in mind. We cover many of the Australian animals that grace this land, animals that put fear into those early Chinese visitors. Also covered is the relationship between the early Chinese and the first Australians (the Australian Aboriginals) and the partnerships they had in friendship, business and marriage…. In addition, of course, we look at some of the Chinese reformers. It is of racialism and compassion, of poverty and riches, but most of all it is about the people. Australian people. Chinese people. Chinese-Australians. Nor could we forget the Chinese mother working long hours so her son or daughter can be educated, the Chinese student, Chinese shopkeeper – all who are determined to make a life in Australia for themselves and their family.

For any historian writing about the development of Australia (not that I am a historian, I am just fascinated), it would be incomplete if they did not include the contribution to Australia by Chinese people. In these pages, you will read about the early visits of Chinese people to Australia, and the importation of Chinese labour to Australia throughout the last 300 years.

Some of the topics covered in this book are: the gold rush days, the White Australian Policy, Chinatowns in Australia, Chinese organized Crime, Chinese-Australian arts, Chinese New Year in Australia, Chinese Investment in Australia and of Chinese business, the Chinese contribution to Australia, Chinese-Australian sporting exchanges, Chinese-Australians serving in the Australian armed forces, the story of Wang Cai (an immigrant in the 1850s), Australia in fifty years' time, the Chinese relationship with Indigenous Australians, conducted interviews with Chinese-Australians and much more.

***

My life is one of wandering, and this probably shows in my writing of this book. Although I made it as a lineal as my wandering mind, no doubt that its meander covers seemingly unconnected topics. This book though is not a literary masterpiece, nor is it academic, and much of it is it based on newspaper reports of the periods. When I started to write this, I did not consider myself an expert on Chinese-Australians, and after finishing it, I still do not regard myself and an expert. It is written to entertain and inform. There are no chapters in this book, just topics in no particular order of importance.

I loved writing this book, and when I started out on this journey I never realised how absorbed or how much fun I would have in reading and learning through that research. I loved it because it is about people more than it is about things, and the more I wrote, or the more I researched, and the more interviews I did, the more I became enthralled. Perhaps you will be as enthralled as I was.

Labels

This book is to bring people together, in oneness of the Australian nationality. However, the very fact that I talk about Chinese-Australians, First Nations people, European-Australians or African-Australians means that I am guilty of categorising through labels. It is not my intention to separate heritage through labels and for that I apologise – I do not mean to elevate or devalue any Australian, irrespective of the heritage. Nevertheless, for this book to be effective and to highlight the Chinese contribution to Australia, I do have to talk about heritage through the medium of labels, specifically Chinese-Australians.

Pat Grayson

About Pat Grayson

Pat Grayson has been writing stories for nearly twenty years (with about eight published books). He is also a publisher and so has helped others write their stories. He travels a lot and has five grandkids who he loves to spoil. He owns an old Winnebago (recreational vehicle), which he restored back to the original, doing as much of the work as his skill allowed. Often, in his "Winnie", he will be in Western Australia, Queensland, Victoria or NSW as he travels, writes and runs his business remotely.

His main interest though, are people. This comes out in the pages of this book. Pat loves to go where people are, to watch people. He will go to a café, not for coffee as he does not drink coffee, but he goes to observe people – to observe them, to marvel as to who that person is, and what their life is like. He can see immediately when someone is strong-minded or too strong-minded. He will observe the interaction between a husband and a wife and see if it is a good respectful relationship or one dominated by one of the partners.

Pat loves life and his life. He loves his family and has a wide circle of friends. No wonder this book is about people.

What is an Australian?

When I grew up, in the 1960s, Australians were basically of English stock, with a smattering of Italian, Greek and a European mix. My own heritage is so mixed it would take another book to describe it. Of course, there were also the First Nations People of Australia – sadly, though, they were not included as "regular" Australians, even though they were the first here by some 60,000 years (you will read more about them later). Even today, in 2018, they are still not included in the Constitution of Australia. This is a ridiculous situation and suggests that Australia has not moved away from the colonial mentality that brought us here over 300 years ago.

Chinese-Australians are one of the largest group of Chinese people living outside of China, and, Australia has more people of Chinese heritage than any other country outside of Asia. That is understandable in some respects because in the grand scheme of things, Australia and China are relatively close neighbours. This is good for Australia, as immigrants from China have settled in virtually every country of the world.

In the 2016 census, Chinese ancestry made up 5.6% of the Australian population. Yet, their influence is probably greater than 5.6% because of their business acumen and also the relationship with China.

There is no doubt that the face of Australia is changing, where roughly 28% of Australians living today were not born in Australia. If we look at the number of people of two generations in Australia (that is people born in Australia but whose parents came from other countries), the figure is close to 60%. When looking at these figures it prompts the question, what is the Australian character?

Later on, I will explain about the Australia White Policy, which gave legislative form to racism. Basically, this was aimed at the Chinese workers. Even though that law literally disintegrated, there are still many here who are xenophobic. The reality is that Australia is the most cosmopolitan country in the world with the largest ratio of immigrants from the largest variety of countries. That is an achievement of which to be proud. I love it when I go down to the local shopping centre or any shopping centre in Australia, and see people from numerous African countries mingling with those from numerous Asian countries, served by people from European countries; taxi drivers from the subcontinent all in clothing that represents their culture, a dozen languages all being spoken at the same time, munching food from an international smorgasbord, and of course the white Australians who have been here for generations. Although different, they all have one thing in common – they are now all Australians and good Australians. The reason why they are good Australians is

According to the Daily Telegraph (*newspaper*) (28 June, 2017) In Sydney there are now more people of Chinese Heritage than people of English heritage.

Australia in the 1840s required labourers, and so the first Chinese workers to come to Australia were indentured labourers. They came to the colony of New South Wales, working mainly on the land as farm hands.

Australia has just celebrated 200 since the first official Chinese migrant came - 1818

The National Museum of Australia
The earliest Chinese contact with Australia appears to have come from fishermen searching the north-western coastline of Australia for sandalwood, bêche-de-mer (trepang) and sea cucumbers. Chinese sources actually refer to a 1477 map that shows the outline of the Australian continent (for them to have had a rough map means that they must have circumnavigated it).

In the journal of HMS Investigator (1802–1803), Matthew Flinders noted that the Aboriginal people of the Gulf of Carpentaria seemed familiar with firearms and iron tools, and he reported seeing pieces of earthen jars, bamboo latticework and other articles, which he thought to be of Chinese origin.

that many have stories to tell. Stories of poverty, stories of war and genocide, stories that I as a middle-class Australian am still horrified at.

There is another aspect that joins them together in a unity of Australianism, and that is they are so grateful to this country for being here, for their opportunities, for their education and that of the children when they had none or very little. These are the very reasons why Australia is lucky to have them – they are the best immigrants that any country could hope to have.

As a third of marriages in Australia happen between people of mixed cultures, across different religions and between different races, with mixes of black and yellow, of fair skinned people with round eyes, almond-shaped eyes, brown eyes, blue eyes, people with crinkly hair or straight, black, blond, red, and in today's world purple, pink and green, and some wearing Hijab and masks. There are others with yarmulkes, while some do tai chi in the park, others on their way to church, or mosque, a temple, or simply to take their children to the park under a stunningly blue sky and silver sun – these are the Australians of today, who will be forging the changing face of Australia and the Australian mentality of the future. Who knows what that face will look like in 500 years' time. I might just stay around to see this.

Australia has always been known as the lucky country, and indeed, it is lucky. It has great mineral wealth, a wonderful climate and the most amazing people that come from the eclectic nations as just described. Because these people have come here, Australia will remain the lucky country, of that I am sure.

There is however, more to consider with what we see in Australia through this mish-mash of humanity, all coalescing, and evolution itself. Australia is one big pot of Australian evolution… Darwin (the famous naturalist), if he was still alive, I am sure would love to write about this coalescing.

***

A report of the time (1950s)
They erected a church for Christian worship in the middle of our Chinatown. This is for the purpose of trying to make us Chinese Christians.

Within history, one cannot separate colonialism and Christian religion, the two went hand in hand, each leveraging off the other. With colonialism, there was always invasion and dominance of the people of the land the colonisers wanted to take control. A prominent tool of invasion and dominance was Christianity in all its various guises. In fact, it could be said with conviction that Christianity was one of the strongest tools for invasion and dominance. So it was the same with the Chinese people, where Christianity lobbied for all sorts of laws to "bring the heathen in line", to dominate, suppress, and control, and to have pennies put in plates.

Nevertheless, to be fair there was also the charitable side of the various Christian religions as they did their best to help support the Chinese people. Many Chinese converted to Christianity. Some because they felt they, or their children, would be better accepted. Others did because they had in fact been converted and wanted to follow the light of Christ.

Fair Dunkum
The two words fair dinkum is synonymous with Australian slang and is believed to have been coined on the Australian goldfields. The *Sydney Morning Herald* (1984) ran a story which suggested that in the early days of Australia, Chinese gold miners used the term din gum, which in their dialect meant 'real gold' when they found gold. Yet, another story says fair dinkum comes from one of the Chinese dialects widely spoken at the diggings; *din* and *kum* – loosely translated as 'true gold'. Moreover, developing to fair dinkum, that my friend is dinkum, pure gold!

Although a lucky country, the climate, at times and in places, is amongst the harshest in the world. Most of Australia is desert or arid at best. It is only the coastal fringe where there is good, consistent rain. The temperature often passes 50 degrees centigrade, and many parts of Australia will be in drought, whilst others are flooded. Not to mention the hundreds of raging bush fires, that sometimes have a front of one hundred kilometres wide. Then up north, every year there are an average of thirteen cyclones a year.

All the major cities are situated in the coastal belt, housing some eighty-five percent of the population. The rest of the coastal belt populates another 10%. Therefore, the interior regions, "the outback" contains roughly .02 people per square kilometre.

***

Chinese people who have taken up home in Australia are approximately 1.4 million in number and comprise of the largest number of Chinese people living in any country outside of Asia. Chinese Australians make up the third largest number of recent immigrants to Australia.

***

As two countries, it is probable that Australia and China will move closer in trade and friendship in the coming years. It is a relationship built on mutual support and geographical expediency. Yet, each is a sovereign state and therefore there will be differences of opinions on occasions. I think the need of each for the other is too great to let those differences of opinion effect the relationship. Perhaps it is like a wife and husband, both supporting the overall relationship whilst retaining their individuality.

It was forty-five years ago when Australia was one of the first countries to recognise the People's Republic of China in friendship and agreement by signing a trade accord. In those days, it would never be envisioned that the current $90 billion of trade a year is a result of that accord.

The average Chinese-Australians of this country, they do not concern themselves with political dealings and are more focused in the day-to-day improvement of life, both here and in China.

NASA data shows that on average, there are 4,595 bush fires per week across Australia.

Australia is the largest island in the world, the smallest continent, and the sixth largest nation by land mass.

With its sparse population of only three per square kilometer (on average), it has the fourth lowest population per square kilometer behind Western Sahara, Suriname and Mongolia. Compare this with the Dongcheng District of China at 22.635 people per square kilometer.

Many early Chinese migrants brought Chinese (coins) currency. This was of no use within the official currency, but used widely within Chinese communities, as their own separate currency.

The early Chinese immigrants referred to Australia as "Jade and Gold", meaning a place of prosperity.

I wonder if the same still applies now.

When in China, many of my friends want to know what I liked the most about their country. Some asked, 'Was it the Great Wall? 'No' I replied, 'that was wonderful'. 'What about the Forbidden City?' they tried. 'Also no,' was my reply. Getting worried they ask, 'Then what have been the best things you have seen?' 'Ahhhh, now you ask the right question… it was the people. They are the best thing that I see in China. All those things you asked about are great, and so full of history, but they are just things. People are not things, they are real…. You are real, and so am I. Feelings and perceptions are more important than buildings and bridges. Mothers are more important than Great Walls or buildings. People are always more important than things.'

Supporting this, as I had another passport photo for my next Chinese visa, the white-Australian who took the photo said, 'Have you been to China before? The people are just so lovely'.

The Gold Rush

In 1851, Edward Hargraves came back to Australia after trying his luck in the gold rush of California. Having been to Bathurst in NSW, he believed that the geology was much the same as in California. With nothing to lose, he sought gold and found it. Once word got out, people from all over the world descended on that pretty mountain area of the Great Dividing Range. It was a bitterly cold place in winter, with high temperatures in summer. They came to seek their fortunes, or rather, to relieve the misery of the poverty that 95% of the world's populous was embroiled in.

Soon thereafter, Thomas Hiscock found gold in Ballarat in Victoria and so hordes of hopefuls also descended there.

Some 40,000 Chinese men came to Australia in the early gold rush days and they referred to Australia as the new Gold Mountain (Dai Gum Son), and so they came to find their fortune. Most came from the Pearl River Delta in southern China, which was an impoverished area. It is understandable that they came as the area was plagued by environmental, economic and political difficulties. They were desperate to do whatever it took to try to improve the life of their families.

Young Chinese men, still living within the parental home, and therefore with the traditional honour and respect, were often forced to go to Australia to help the family escape the rounds of poverty. The young men felt it their duty to comply. Many were enticed by the promise of gold. Most were men who had been contracted by agents, and who sponsored their voyage. As a result, they faced more years of poverty whilst they made the repayments. The agents were Chinese and often made a fortune. Sadly, though, many of the young hopefuls died on the way to Australia, and many also died as they were making their way from their ship drop-off points to the various goldfields, as the land and climate was too harsh. The number of deaths is not known as the lands they crossed were vast and settlements few. It was not only the Chinese who died, migrants from all over the world sustained deaths in the same way.

Wherever gold was found, people came in such numbers that bustling townships sprung up, literally overnight. In most instances, services, such as garbage collection or road works, could not keep up. Indeed, these were wild places.

Many of the newspaper reports of the early Australian days use the term Celestial when referring to the Chinese people. Throughout this book, within old newspaper reports, you will see the term Celestial.

The term derived from Pinyin's (dialect) Tianchao, which translated to Celestial Empire. So the term celestial or celestials had been used for Chinese people, especially in newspaper reporting.

Of Chinese kindness in Australia
In the 1870s, an article in The Advertiser titled, "A Generous Chinaman"

A few days ago, during the heavy rain and piercing winds, a poor woman has been observed passing up Herbert Street with an infant in her arms and another unfortunate child clinging to her skirt. Heaven knows where she was straying but her appearance was that of abject poverty. A few persons were looking on with pity when a Celestial was observed to hurry from his place of business with a large parcel which he gave to the woman, and at once returned to his store. The parcel proved to be a pair of superior blankets. The gift was made in a quiet manner without the slightest ostentation, that it took those who witnessed it by surprise. The donor was **Sun Tong Lee**, *a Chinese merchant in this town, and this generous action is in the highest degree creditable to his humanity.*

In one year alone (1857) 205464 ounces of gold (that is around 259 million UD dollars in today's prices found its way back to China. They also shipped back vast sums of money that they made from wages or their various businesses.

The wives and children of these Chinese migrants were not allowed to go with their men. One reason was that they were (to a degree) retained as ransom so the young man would come back. Another reason was, that money was not to be wasted on the sending a mere woman.

Some of the Chinese made money, not on the mines, but on supporting services, such as merchants, farmers, or the less salubrious brothels and opium dens. Most however, nearly starved to death on the small amount they made after deducting for the agent's fee. In most cases though, what little they made, a good portion was sent to their family in the villages in China. To stop themselves from starvation, the Chinese worked jobs the Europeans did not want to do. These jobs did not require the ability to speak English, and more often than not, they were underpaid.

From the Culture Victoria website – This photograph is believed to have been taken of a coach in Newstead, near Castlemaine on its way to Fiddlers Creek. Fiddler's Creek was the site of an alluvial rush in 1853. The coach is overflowing with Chinese miners and luggage. Note the Chinese-style hats on back of coach. Might there be a phrasebook in some of that luggage? These are likely to be "free paying passengers". (Image out of copyright)

Chinese workers, mostly men, came to Australia to try their luck in the gold fields. By this time, it was seldom that alluvial gold was found as most had been already mined. Now the larger companies with greater funding were required to mine at deeper depths.

Most of the Chinese workers were from the southern part of China, and by 1861 there were over 24, 000 Chinese on the Victorian goldfields. They came to make their fortune, and return to China as rich men. However, for most, it did not work out that way because most were indebted to Chinese businessman for their travel costs to Australia, and so they had to work long hard hours to pay this off before they could return home. Nevertheless, some 4,000 remained in Australia either by choice or because they could not raise the money to get home, or because of death.

There was great hardship on the goldfields, where something like 90% of the people were from other countries. There was rivalry and fighting between all the racial groups and racism was rife. The Chinese were subject to a lot of abuse from the workers because of their yellow skin. At one stage, a large band of workers attacked the Chinese quarter with many people injured. But it would have been worse if the troops had not arrived to stop the attack. None of the attackers were prosecuted, which shows the sentiment against the Chinese people at that time.

From the National Museum of Australia
The Chinese Furniture Trade

The move by Chinese immigrants into furniture making had its beginnings in the gold rush days when Chinese miners made wooden boxes to transport gold back to China. Their furniture, often made from rattan and Australian cedar, appealed to people on limited incomes both for its price and contemporary style. Rattan is a pliable palm, soaked in water so it can be easily shaped into cane furniture.

Lonsdale, Little Lonsdale and Exhibition streets in Melbourne were the centers of the Chinese furniture trade. Some 175 Chinese firms could be found along these streets.

Pressure from other furniture-makers to curtail expansion of the Chinese furniture trade brought about the Factories and Shops Act, passed by the governments of both Victoria and New South Wales in 1896. All Chinese-made furniture had to be stamped with the words "Chinese labour". The legislation also regulated the definition of a factory; whereas a minimum of four Europeans were considered to constitute a factory, one Chinese person could not be legally considered a factory.

During the depression of the 1890s, many Chinese cabinet-makers lost their jobs and turned to running laundries. In a few years, almost every suburb in Melbourne had its own Chinese laundry. In 1913, 31 per cent of Victorian laundry workers were Chinese, compared with less than 5 per cent in New South Wales where, despite less stringent regulations, they failed to attract significant custom from the Anglo-Australian community.

The Argus (newspaper), 13th of October 1859

The fearful number of fateful accidents among our Chinese mining population calls for some preventative, if it can be devised.

Last week three unfortunate Celestials were killed on Campbell's Creek, and the whole of these casualties might have been avoided with ordinary care. The Chinese will not timber their holes like the Europeans, and hence the frequent cases of violent death among the former. It is a common remark amongst miners that the Chinese will work where Europeans will not, and that no European will encounter the risk incurred by the Chinese. However, it is much easier to point out the evil than to devise a remedy for it.

It must have been a tremendously difficult time for those workers, working long hours for very little pay, in a strange land where people were antagonistic to them, and of course, there were virtually no Chinese women with whom to console themselves. The eligible white women frowned upon the Chinese men, and would not lower themselves to go with men whom they called "coolies".

After the frenzy of the gold rush, most of the people dispersed from the goldfields, and the few Chinese that remained in Australia, or rather the territories, moved into other ventures in the major cities such as gardeners, restaurateurs and shopkeepers. Whatever money they earned they sent back to their families in China.

Report from the *Argus (newspaper)*, 7 May 1861

They (the Chinese miners) excavate a large paddock, in many instances 60 to 70 ft, and all the dirt from the surface to the wash dirt is removed by these industrious miners in buckets slung on bamboo up a flight of stairs cut in the corner or the centre of the excavation, and it is then piled up at some distance from the scene of their labours in huge mounds resembling miniature mountains. In many instances, I saw hills of mullock twenty feet high. By this mode or operation, they can work the ground without timbering, as all the dirt taken out is removed far enough to present its weight forcing in the sides of the cutting. The European miners seem to have taken the hint, and are commencing work on a similar plan, only substituting wheelbarrows for the buckets and the bamboos…

The Argus *(newspaper)*, 19 June 1862

A writer in our daily news visited the Chinese camp where he was treated with great kindness and hospitality. The conversation turned upon the vast quantity spurious (suspect) gold weekly offered for sale in town. (The conversation turned to the manufacturing of gold, which clearly can't be done)… Ah-Loo laughed at what he called my simplicity and told me that … …Chinamen manufactured large specimen nuggets… … the Chinese are a little ingenious. We take, for example, five ounces of genuine gold, five ounces of brass, and two ounces of zinc, melt them in a common pot, pour the mixture into a mould – you have now a bar of gold. Take a file or rasp, and file away until you have reduced it to powder – i.e., spurious fine gold; mix it in the proportion of two to three with fine gold, and sell it.

Just a few weeks after being sworn in as Prime Minister, Gough Whitlam (1972), embarked on furthering diplomatic relations with the People's Republic of China. This was an important period in the China and Australian trade and relations.

The first Chinese ambassador to Australia was His Excellency Wang Guoquan. Conversely, when Australian's first ambassador to China departed for China, there were about six hundred Chinese-Australians there to see him off.

White Australia Policy (Racialism – fear of foreigners)

The early days of Chinese migration to Australia

In the early days of this land, there was no such country called Australia. However, there were (ultimately) six sovereign British colonies, all responsible to the British Crown. These were: Tasmania, New South Wales, Victoria, and later on Western Australia, Queensland, then last was the Northern Territory. Australia became an independent country (Federation) in January 1901 after the British Parliament passed legislation allowing the six Australian colonies (and later the Australian Capital Territory {ACT}) to govern in their own right as part of the Commonwealth of Australia.

Before 1901, two of these sovereign colonies, Victoria and New South Wales, legislated to control the number of Chinese people coming in to settle. These also were the two colonies where gold was first discovered. The main control of access was at the various ports. Ever resourceful though, the Chinese went by boat to other colonies, such as South Australia and hiked over the border in the dry and sparsely populated country.

Xenophobia has been rife for thousands of years, and it was no different in the early days of Australia. There are many reasons why the people of a country fear people from other countries. The main reason though is ignorance. At the time, the white people in Australia would have said that they worried that the cheaper wages that were paid to the Chinese labourers would undermine their own earnings. In addition, people, especially in those days worried about a race that looked different to themselves. They felt that they were superior and so did not want to "be contaminated" by yellow skin, and that the culture was too alien. Moreover, so there was much antagonism against the Chinese people, and that there were many anti-Chinese demonstrations. Many ended in bloodshed.

Australian nationalism was growing in this young nation, and the people craved a national identity – and Chinese, or black people were not going to be a part of this. Various colonial parliaments imposed more and more restrictions. In 1888, about thirty-thousand Australians attended an anti-Chinese rally in Sydney, organised by the anti-Chinese League. The various newspapers supported the sentiment, thereby increasing the racial tension.

The result of all of this became known as The White Australia Policy, which continued until well after federation of the colonies into one country – Australia. In fact, is was the fear of different coloured foreigners that

For Chinese readers Although Australia is a sovereign country with a Federal government, each state or territory, such as N.S.W and Tasmania, has its own state government. This is a hang-up of the independent British colonies that comprised the land. Some Australians, and certainly the State and Territory governments, will tell you it is a good thing for the people of their own state or territory (of course each state government wants to retain their own power position). The reality is that it is expensive and clumsy. Imagine a system where virtually every single law in the land is re written or reinterpreted eight different times for each of the states and territories, and again for the Federal government.

To try and escape some of the racialism, many of the Chinese changed their names to Western names, cut their tails (long hair), and dressed as Westerners.

They forced their children, not to just go to school, but to excel at school.

From the National Museum of Australia
The worst violence against Chinese miners was in central New South Wales. European diggers were incensed by the Chinese and their apparent wastage of water when extracting gold. A weak police presence was unable to contain the situation. Six anti-Chinese riots occurred at the Lambing Flat camps over a period of ten months. The most serious riot occurred on 14 July 1861 when approximately 2,000 European diggers attacked the Chinese miners. Although they tried to get away from the violent mob, about 250 Chinese miners were gravely injured and most lost all their belongings. After this tragic event, Lambing Flat was renamed Young.

It was not all bad... James Roberts and his family gave refuge to many injured Chinese miners on their property just outside the Back Creek goldfields. Over the course of a few weeks, about 1200 Chinese refugees arrived at the Roberts station (farm). In helping the injured Chinese miners, the Roberts family risked having their produce boycotted and being attacked themselves by angry mobs.

was a uniting factor of all the colonies, where they felt, combined as one nation, they would be able to better "keep out" any who were not white.

From the National Archives of Australia website, research by Kate Bagnal:
> The records document(ed) *many aspects of the lives of Chinese Australians, including immigration and travel, business enterprises, political activities and community life. The records are a legacy of the discrimination and marginalisation of the White Australia years, but* (now) *they can be used by researchers to recover the lives of Chinese Australians in the past, and also to provide a more nuanced understanding of the contradictions and complications of Australia's response to its Chinese population.*

From the National Archives of Australia, below is some text on what was known as the *The Poon Gooey case of 1910–13*:
> *A good illustration of this policy; to further reduce the Chinese presence in Australia. In the records of the Poon Gooey case, and many others like it, we can see how Chinese people found themselves at odds with the official policies that governed their lives in Australia. Centred around the deportation of Ham Hop, the wife of Poon Gooey, the case focused attention on the limitations placed on the entry of Chinese wives, and highlighted to many white Australians the inhumanity of the White Australia Policy when it was strictly applied to otherwise good, decent people. Australia's Chinese community, like many around the world, had historically been one predominantly of men. When Ham Hop arrived in Australia as Poon Gooey's wife in 1910, he became one of only 801 Chinese men who had their wives living with them in Australia and Ham Hop was one of only 181 Chinese-born wives of Chinese men in the country. The Australian government was keen that these sorts of numbers should not increase... and a baby daughter, Queenie Hop Poon Gooey, was born at Geelong on 5 June 1911. Further extensions of Ham Hop's exemption certificate were granted, and a second daughter, Lena Hop Poon Gooey, was born on 4 January 1913. Growing increasingly reluctant to allow Ham Hop to remain in Australia any longer, the government threatened deportation and the family eventually left Melbourne for China in May 1913. Ham Hop's original stay of six months had grown to two and a half years.*

> *The Commonwealth government was reluctant to set a precedent by allowing Ham Hop to remain in Australia, fearing that such action would lead to an increase in the Chinese population. Many ordinary Australians, however, felt the injustice that was being perpetrated by not allowing the family of Poon Gooey, a respectable, Christian businessman, to live with him in Australia. Many also believed that he had been naturalised, while his two children were certainly Australian-born British subjects. The Christian churches vocally supported Poon Gooey's efforts to keep his family with him, as did various other groups. Petitions*

Even though there was legislation to stop Chinese men from bringing their wives, some did, and some got through. Some of these people had children of their own. When those children grew up, they wanted to marry a Chinese born girl – but they couldn't, they were not allowed to bring her into the country.

The *Argus (newspaper)*, 7 November 1857
It also becomes an interesting subject of enquiry to what extent it is desirable to continue a crusade against these people, and whether it would not be better to encourage their settlement here to some extent rather than compel them, by unkind treatment and hard legislation, to go home laden with the gold of this country. The storekeepers and merchants, also of whose goods the Chinese are great consumers, would be the first to feel their loss were they to leave the country in great numbers.

As reported in the Argus *(newspaper)*, 11th October 1860
A Chinaman had gone to a camp of his countrymen and stole a blanket and a pair of trousers. A hue and cry was once given, and ten of them ran howling in chase, and soon caught the poor man, whom they punished according to their own fashion, he being dragged along the ground by his tail (hair), kicked and dreadfully beaten with bamboo sticks. Later, he was tied by the hair tail of his head to a stake, and suffering greatly…. (and later still) probably with the loss of his tail, which too many Chinese, is punishment as severe as the loss of either an eye or limb.

The following is from a review of the book *Big White Lie* by John Fitzgerald. The review was written by MD Brady on the site Library Things.

As Fitzgerald explains, Australians were narrow-minded in defining themselves and excluding Chinese by declaring that the Chinese lacked particular Australian values of freedom, justice, and "mateship". As their activities show, the Chinese did not lack these values. Countries need to define themselves in universal human terms, not the more limited national ones.

were signed, meetings were held and letters were written, all to no avail. The Chinese community were also active in using the family's situation to agitate for changes to Australia's discriminatory legislation, and the case was reported in the Australian Chinese press. Interestingly, one of the arguments used by both white and Chinese Australians to support Poon Gooey's efforts to have his wife continue to live with him in Australia was a shared opposition to intermarriage and racial mixing.

The Poon Gooey case was a relatively rare moment when the concerns and difficulties faced by a Chinese family in Australia reached the consciousness of the broader Australian community. Because of their interest, and because of Poon Gooey's ongoing efforts to keep his family in Australia...

That was just over one hundred years ago and occasionally, still today, the same issue occurs where a wife or husband is deported from Australia, leaving the rest of the family in Australia. These are now usually refugees.

There was one heartbreaking situation a few years ago where several Muslim teenagers from one family were deported back to the Middle East; whilst the mother was allowed to remain (they went to the estranged father). Two hundred years ago, one hundred years ago, and now, it was and still is a heart-wrenching situation. Like the Poon Gooey case, the outrage from the general population is loud and strong with the injustice and uncompassionate bureaucratic process.

It was only in the 1960s that the White Australian policy was repealed. This is ironic, when one considers that there are really only the original Australians, these being the Australian Ab**originals** – (notice the word original), but they were displaced.

In some ways, it is understandable why there is the sentiment to keep the homogeneity of a race intact. In another sense, all people are a component of hundreds, if not thousands of cultures before them, and all from the original gene pool. Even China has legislated to reduce the European influence on its race (more on this later). The Germans, under Adolf Hitler, rose to power using anti-Semitism, racialism and tried to propagate German Nationalism through retaining the "Master Race" and the "Aryan Race". The First Testament of the Bible teaches that the Jews are the chosen race (of course this is written by the Jewish people). In addition, history reflects the annihilation of many people by Moses and others in their quest to assert the fact that they are the chosen people. We all know about apartheid in South Africa, with the Afrikaners who choose to believe themselves to be "the chosen" people, thereby giving them power to do as they saw fit with the black Africans of the country. In fact, there has probably not been a country that has not tried to retain the purity of their culture. Moreover, although Australia's policies were racialist, never did they legislate genocide, or

The Argus *(newspaper)*, 7 May 1868
Clearly referring to a deceased person. It appears that a fund, contributed to by the greater part of the Chinese residents of the colony, is in existence, and devoted to the defraying (paying) of expenses incurred either in the exhumation (the digging up a of a buried corpse) or preservation of the remains of deceased Chinaman for transmission to the flowery land... Accordingly, a coffin of the ordinary shape was made of the zinc, to fit into one made of wood, in the former of which the remains of the defunct (dead) celestial were deposited, and the lid soldered on, and an opening being left for the introduction of fourteen gallons of brandy. This having been affected the double coffin and its contents were placed in a case made of cedar and New Zealand pine, secured with batons, the corners being firmly bound with iron bands. The case was duly polished and delivered to the countryman of the deceased, who, by permission of the coroner, forthwith removed it to Ballarat en route to China.

More taxes – In 1859 the Victorian Government placed a tax of ten pounds to slow the rate of Chinese arrivals. So many of the men landed in Robe or Port Adelaide in South Australia to avoid the Victorian tax. However, they had to walk the eight-hundred kilometres (approximate) to Bendigo. At twenty miles a day, it took about forty days of difficult walking. Sometimes they negotiated with Aboriginals to take them.

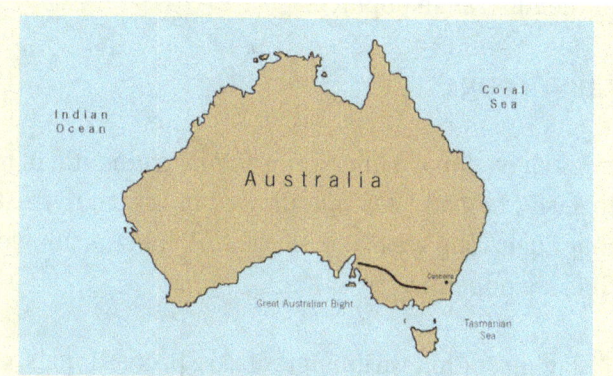

Walking from Port Adelaide to Bendigo (approximately 800 kilometers)

The Australian (national) newspaper is one of the largest by circulation in the country. The Chinese version only started twelve months ago and its uptake has been phenomenal, with over one million subscribers reading the Chinese version.

The first Chinese consulate opened in Melbourne in 1909.

allow genocide to occur, other than with the Australian Aboriginals, where they almost succeeded in the elimination of that race of people.

Over time however, Australians grew more compassionate, and knew that they could not keep their borders closed to immigrants of colour – too many were coming from countries in turmoil. In 1965, the governing party overrode the racial policy. Thereafter, 9,000 non-whites were allowed to immigrate to Australia, and the numbers have grown. In 1989, the then Australian Minister Bob Hawke, allowed 42,000 Chinese students to immigrate to Australia. Many of those are now married and have had children in Australia.

Now, in 2018, to my way of thinking, the Australian government, and the various state governments, have been proactive in welcoming and supporting new Chinese Australians. And yes, there are times when bureaucracy gets in the way, but from a legislative point of view, Australia is trying to do well by our legislative framework. Of course there are still parochial views and racism, but that is really only from a small portion of the Australian populous.

Chee Tong

It is believed that a Chee Tong was instrumental in helping to ease the law when it came to Chinese migration. In 1947, he had been not allowed to return to Australia, after arriving here earlier. Scanned records reveal that Chee Tong was later successful in being allowed to re-enter the country. This opened the door to other Chinese hopefuls.

Today, most Chinese immigrants are professionals, scholars, doctors, business investors and IT specialists, etc.

Historical Chinese Xenophobia

It would seem that the Australian Government was racially motivated and treated the Chinese harshly. Perhaps they did, and yes, they had their prejudices. Nevertheless, at the same time history shows that the various Chinese governments/emperors over the centuries have been equally determined to keep out foreigners and to stop the foreigners from tainting their blood. It is a natural thing to be patriotic in the country of one's birth, and we all fear change, even though that change can bring benefit. So one can't blame the Chinese emperors or the Australian Government from being overzealous in this regard.

I got the following from Wikipedia and what it shows is the control that the Qing Government tried to employ to keep China pure.

> ... From the system's inception in 1757, trading in China was extremely lucrative for European and Chinese merchants alike as goods such as tea, porcelain, and silk were valued highly enough in Europe to justify the expenses of traveling to Asia. The system was highly regulated by the Qing government. Foreign traders were only permitted to do business through a body of Chinese merchants known as the Cohong, and were forbidden to learn Chinese. Foreigners could only live in one of the Thirteen Factories (a neighbourhood along the Pearl River) and were not allowed to enter or trade in any other part of China, a policy the Qing called the *Yī kǒu tōngshāng* (口通商), or the "Single port commerce system". Only low level government officials could be dealt with, and the imperial court could not be lobbied for any reason excepting official diplomatic missions. The Imperial laws that upheld the system were collectively known as the Prevention of Barbarian Ordinances (防范外夷規條.)

The Prevention Of the Barbarian Ordinance seems similar to the White Australia policy, and is likely to have been administered with the same lack of compassion, as displayed in the Poon Gooey case.

In China, from the time the first Europeans arrived in 100AD-166AD there was trade between Romano

In Darwin, in 1886 there were roughly 4,000 Chinese, mainly men. About 2000 of these were used to construct the rail line from Darwin to Pine Creek (gold had been found at Pine Creek). The distance of the line of approximately 248 kilometers took three years. The work was backbreaking, and with the high temperatures of the top end of Australia, and long days it must have been unbearably tough. This, apparently, was the only railway line in Australia built with Chinese labour.

Henry Lawson was one of Australia's most famous authors. He is loved for his prose about early Australia and those hardy people who shaped Australia. In his *Christmas in the Goldfields* (around 1908), Lawson reminisced about those days and referred to **Sun Tong Lee** as "Santa Claus... as a Chinaman with strange and delicious sweets that melted in our mouths and rum toys and Chinese dolls for the children..."

and China. In 1266 Maffeo Polo of Italy arrived and from then on, there were many more. Even so, the Chinese, and the various emperors were cautious with limiting trade and immigration from the Europeans to China. However, being pragmatic, they tried to learn as much from the foreigners as possible. However, they also wanted to limit foreign religions from "indoctrinating" (Guanshu) the people. This situation remained in place for several hundred years, and was only relaxed from 1990 onwards.

Yu Hai of the Department of Sociology, Fudan University, gave a speech called *Racism and Xenophobia in China to Casa Asia*. At one point he states ... (As reflected on **www.highbeam.com**)... Like most other countries in the world, China is also afflicted with racism and xenophobia. Take for instance those Chinese cities we may have had the chance to encounter black people. Discrimination and even disparagement targeted against black people are usually unveiled and undisguised...

... However, entrenched in the long history of China has been xenophobia, which legitimises discrimination or even hostility against other races based on Sinocentrism...

This kind of cultural superiority is embedded in historical discourse... Moreover, later Europeans were known as the long nosed people (long noses were horrible to the Chinese people).

Much research has shown me that from inception, Chinese people rejected Christianity and resented missionaries in China, and that the Chinese regarded anyone who lived outside of China as a savage or a barbarian. Europeans, for example, ... "have more hair than monkeys, large ears and noses like anteaters, and smell more awful than dead bodies." The Chinese believed "some white people tied themselves together to keep them from being snatched away by eagles, and others had holes in their chest so they could be carried by poles." According to one account, some towns in Europe were composed entirely of woman who became pregnant by staring at their shadow, and one Chinese proverb states, "We can fool any foreigner." At one stage, inviting a foreigner into one's home or accepting foreign currencies, were crimes that could land one in prison.

Fortunately, for most countries, including Australia and China, the racialism as first legislated is now a thing of the past – most people live with compassion for their fellow man, irrespective of race, creed or colour.

***

A Nation of Ideals

I would like to finish this chapter by saying that Australians of today are a nation with ideals of equality. Yes, there are elements in our society, as there are in all societies, who are xenophobic and are in fear of anyone who is not like them. This is unfortunate and usually is a result of fear based in ignorance and culture.

Australia does not have one piece of legislation that discriminates against any of our immigrants. I have mentioned that our legislation is not as inclusive for the First Australian people as it should be, and that is not good, but that is not what I am referring to here. The various governments do their best to encourage and help our immigrants. We may not be able to stop a xenophobic from an act of hate, but he or she is usually caught, fined or jailed – there are laws in place to protect all from racial acts. In addition, although our past has not been squeaky clean, we can be proud of the egalitarian infrastructure that has developed.

Most Australians are essentially supportive of all colours and extend a hand of friendship when needed. They are generous with their help and the giving of money when called upon to do so (see below). I am proud of being Australian, and feel that most of us have the right attitude to our fellow humans, irrespective of their colour.

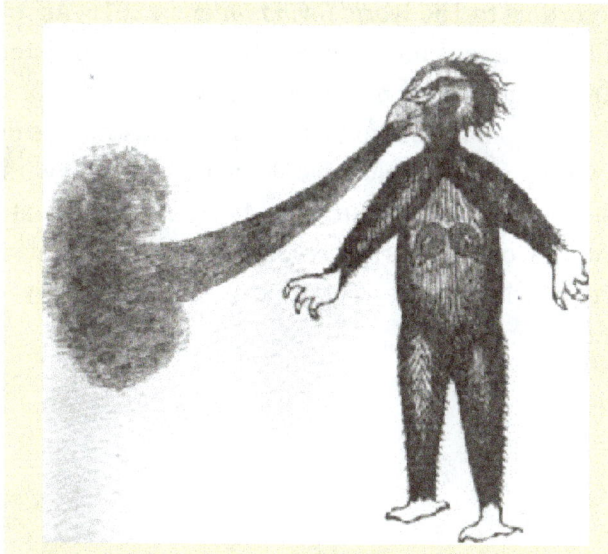

Barbarian, as seen by the early Chinese

Referring to the Confucian tradition…

They do not share the same blood as we do, so they must be different from us in nature. Nevertheless, Confucius referred to anyone not Chinese as barbarians … and that… The Chinese race is superior, deriving from our cultural superiority… …

According to The *World Giving Index*, in 2016, Australians were the third most generous nation for giving to aid foundations and charities (the ratio is consistent with previous years). One site I looked at stated that 80% of Australians have given freely to a charity or a not-for-profit organisation over the last twelve months. The Australian government says that Australians donate about $4 billion per year to good causes, and the government themselves would be less efficient without all the volunteer organisations. The 2015 report for the organisation *Volunteering Australia* stated that 36.2% of Australians participated in some form of voluntary work in a formal setting. There are also many who are not in the formal setting, such as community groups who may clean up a local picnic area or river, so the figure is likely to be over 40% of Australian voluntary work.

From the National Museum of Australia

To mark the Chinese Revolution in 1911, the Dragon flag, the symbol of the Qing (Manchu) dynasty, was replaced with the twelve-pointed star republican flag at the Chinese Consulate-General in Melbourne. Chinese-Australian born William Liu an interpreter at the Consulate, was charged with pulling down the Manchu flag and hoisting the new republican flag.

The revolution was met with a mixed reaction by Chinese communities in Australia. Although many rejoiced at the demise of the Manchu dynasty and celebrated with myriads of fireworks, the more conservative Chinese communities organised a Dragon flag parade in Sydney to demonstrate their support for the Imperial dynasty.

The Chinese Museum in Melbourne

Chinese music was bought to Australia by goldminers in the 1850s. Cantonese opera was the main source of music and entertainment and a great source of spiritual education for the Chinese miners. It also provided an important place to socialise and the means for self-expression, Chinese Opera was performed in gambling houses and for occasional festivals ceremonies and charity occasions.

The first miss Chinatown Contest (Melbourne) was in 1961.

They Came – Early Chinese immigrants to Australia

Mei Quong Tart, hero and gentleman from China

The following story of Mei Quong Tart is my story, but the facts are based on numerous newspaper cuttings, of which many are listed in the bibliography.

Quong Tart (as Mei Guangda) was born at Sunning in China's Canton province in 1850. His father was a merchant of some note. This suggests that he was of middle-class extraction. Little did anybody know at that stage that Tart was highly intelligent and of exceptional character. I am sure that his father would have been proud of him.

But he was to leave his father and family as the opportunity came for the young Tart. At nine years old, he travelled with his uncle to Australia. They were part of a group of Chinese men who came to work on the goldfields in NSW of Australia.

One wonders at the spectacle of all these Chinese men going to the distant land that was so different in culture from their own land (refer to the story further on in the book of Wang Cai). Most would have gone in the hope and need of making money to send back to their loved ones in their home villages. Filled with adventure and selflessness to support their families, they also would have carried uncertainty for this new and strange land. Nevertheless, they also carried the love of their tradition – would they ever see their villages and family again? What would nine year old Tart have thought as he walked up that gangplank carrying his meagre possessions. He probably would have been younger than most, perhaps confident and a bit cheeky – that is what he would have looked like on the outside. On the inside, he would have been sad at leaving his mother, father and siblings for an unknown land.

When arriving, Tart had no English but it was reported that only a few years later he was able to act as an interpreter between English speaking people of Australia and the Chinese. This indicates that from an early age, his ability to earn money and see opportunities came naturally to him. It is also indicative of his intelligence.

Those days must have been exciting, and hard, but the young Chinese man was known to be wealthy by the time he was eighteen years of age. But I am ahead of the story. Sometime after arriving in Australia, he found

Australian Prime ministers

Kevin Rudd served twice as Australian Prime Minister (from December 2007 to June 2010, and again from June to September 2013). He was proficient in Mandarin and all state visits/discussions to China or with the Chinese personal was in Mandarin.

The current Prime minister, Malcolm Turnbull has extended family with Chinese heritage.

Quong Tart - image in Melbourne Chinese Museum

Quong Tart, successful businessman outside one of his tearooms. Image courtesy of the City of Sydney and Australian Society of Genealogists PR6-26-14.

himself on the property of a Mr. and Mrs. Percy Simpson, who originally were from Scotland. The Simpsons had mining leases, and that is where Tart worked and learnt his trade.

One assumes that the young Tart worked hard and was well liked by the Simpsons, as after hours, Mrs. Simpson helped to educate him and trained him how to be a gentleman. I wonder why he was chosen or did the compassionate Mrs. Simpson want to help as many as possible? Surely though, he would have been a willing and intelligent student. So on the one hand, he had an education and read many fine books of literature, yet, he would have had the experience of life, working with rogues, thieves, drunkards, poets, and the educated – people from all over the world – all gained at an early age.

At eighteen, with a fortune under his belt made by investing in gold claims (he probably watched and learnt from Mr. Simpson), he employed around two hundred Chinese and Europeans workers as he continued to grow his fortune on the goldfields. However, as a gentleman with money and more leisure, he also pursued sporting endeavours, such as cricket and football. Apparently, he did very well at both and was probably the first Chinese person to play either. One can see him as a cosmopolitan man, encased in all the modern garments of the time, where he had one foot in the Chinese camp of his heritage and the other in the European camp, his chosen home – but he was accepted and loved by both.

On his first visit back to China (Tart was known to have gone back to China numerous times), whilst visiting his family, and wanting to expand his business, he went into a partnership with his brother who ran Loong Shan tea plantation. Upon returning to Sydney he opened a business as a tea and silk merchant. It was not long before he had a string of teashops. His next venture was in creating alcoholic beverages, which were also sold in his refreshment houses.

In 1871 he became a naturalised Australian, and, along the way, on the 30th August 1886 he married a young English school teacher, Margaret Scarlett, the daughter of George Scarlett, a station (farm) master. This upset Tart's mother who had been busy selecting potential girls in China to be his wife. Tart, by that time had become very much Westernised and believed that a "well-appointed" European wife would help serve his personal and business needs better than a girl from the homeland.

However, it was not only Tart's mother who was upset. So was Margaret's father, George Scarlett. His Scottish stubbornness never relented, he refused to go to the wedding, and virtually disowned his daughter. When he died, Margaret was the only child to have been left out of his will. Not only that, reports indicate that he was not a good grandfather to his grandchildren and kept his distance from them. This is a shame because one of the greatest gifts in life are our grandchildren (I have five so I should know), and one of the greatest gifts a child can have is a loving and fun grandfather.

Marrying Tart must have been a courageous act, as EJ Lea-Scarlett records indicated; Margaret was fully aware of her father's intolerant attitude to inter-racial marriage. Margaret, by all accounts was supportive of Tart in all that he did, and was a great confidante, shrewd in her own way. Moreover, even though her father distanced her, she never wavered in her support for Tart.

Never forgetting the difficulties of trying to earn a living in those difficult early days, with so much poverty and hardship, it was from this position that his generosity of spirit to all those battlers of life emerged. There are literally dozens of newspaper cuttings that reported his generosity in supporting yet, another good cause. Most of his financial support went to his own Chinese people. Nevertheless, he supported many causes, any that could help people. Nor did he forget the Australian Aboriginals, where his generosity towards these displaced people is also recorded. I believe that he saw in the Australian Aboriginals a race of people who had so much to offer but were legislated and bullied into submission. Apparently, it was Tart who first referred to the Aboriginals as the 'original owners' of the land – the term is widely accepted by our First Nations people.

Perhaps his biggest individual contribution was to fund the building of a public school in Bell's Creek. This was an inter-denominational church school.

It is said that in those goldfields areas that he operated, there was relative peace between the Chinese and the European miners, mainly because of Tart's positive influence. He was wise and well respected by both sides, and mediated on many issues.

With the growth of his wealth, and his benevolence towards society, so his fame grew. Newspaper reports suggested that, "Quong Tart is as well-known as the Governor himself, and is quite as popular among all classes."

The document, *The Chinese Experience in Australia – A Brief Outline for Stages 3–5*, stated, "When he threw open the doors of his large new premises (a tea room) in King Street at the end of 1889, the man who performed the actual official opening was none other than Sir John Robertson. The King Street tearooms had a reading and writing room upstairs, and the complex was to become a famous meeting and partying place in the city over the ensuing years." It was his grandest tea room with marble fountains and ponds, where golden carp leisurely swam to the amusement of the patrons. The establishment was believed to have employed about fifty people. In addition, later, his Elite Hall in the Queen Victoria Market Building was formally opened by the Mayor of Sydney, Matthew Harris, in 1898.

Sydney News shows that Tart employed at his residence, Gallop House, at least three servants, a nanny, a parlour maid and a gardener.

He also had progressive ideas about Sydney's social scene and politics. His tea rooms were the site of the first meetings of Sydney's suffragettes (woman seeking the vote), and he devised new and improved employment policies for staff, such as paid sick leave. He was a spokesman for the Chinese community, often advocating for the rights of Chinese-Australians, and was one of the founders of the first Chinese merchants association in Sydney, titled the Lin Yik Tong.

As mentioned, he campaigned against the opium trade and its importation into Australia, and its use with the Chinese community, and in 1883, Tart went on an investigation to the Chinese camps in Southern New South Wales to attempt to reduce the use of opium.

On one of Tarts visit to China, in 1894, he was advanced to a *Mandarin of the Fourth Degree*. His love for his homeland never diminished, and it would seem that his homeland's love for him also never diminished.

Unfortunately, on the evening of 19 August 1902, at his office, intruders brutally bashed Tart with an iron bar, wrapped in newspaper, and robbed him of around twenty pounds. This was a large sum of money in those days. The crime shocked the people of Sydney. The assailant, Frederick Duggan, described as a "dim-witted thug" was jailed for twelve years, a light sentence in which the police chose to believe that it was a simple robbery gone wrong. Many however, believed that the beating was arranged by "Western people" or by jealous Chinese businessmen – we will never know.

Although, he seemed to have recovered, he was dead eleven months later from an attack of pleurisy. It seems that it was from his weakened state from the bashing that he succumbed to death. He was fifty-three.

His funeral, which was held on July 23 1903, was like a state funeral, where two hundred Chinese men escorted the coffin from his Ashfield mansion to a train, specifically hired for the funeral, to carry his polished oak coffin. An entire carriage was required to carry the many floral tributes.

Thousands of people, both white and Chinese, lined the rail track to pay their last respects. Tart was dressed in his ceremonial robes of a *Mandarin of the Blue Button*. At the Necropolis, 1,500 mourners marched.

The Reverend Joseph Best read the burial service. However, part of the service was conducted in Chinese by the Reverend Soo Hoo Tan.

The funeral was well covered in many newspapers. *The Advertiser,* for instance wrote, "Few men were so widely known or so much esteemed, his name, indeed, being quite a household word throughout the whole land…"

Merchants of the city, especially the Chinese, shut their businesses for the day as a mark of respect. Flags were at half-mast. Among the messages of sympathy received by Tart's widow, Margaret, were tributes from Sir Henry Rawson – the New South Wales Governor, Sir William Lyne – the former New South Wales Premier and Sir Edmund Barton – Australia's first Prime Minister.

There was much to admire about Tart, but what was it that he was most admired? His intelligence, his business acumen, his generosity and support for the underdog, his ability to carve a niche for himself in Australian history? He was a statesman, and a self-made millionaire. He was a family man and a man of spiritual pursuits. He became an Australian, and loved the land of Australia and the people within it. He supported the Aboriginal cause. He never forgot

Opium

Perhaps because of their loneliness, or because of addiction, many of the Chinese workers indulged in opium smoking. At the time opium was not illegal in the colonies, and so it was bought in large quantities, and opium dens sprung up wherever there were Chinese people. Many destroyed their lives as a result of the habit. This further annoyed the European miners towards the Chinese, as some Europeans also indulged in the habit.

Anti-opium campaigns were conducted as well as organisations set up (simular to anti-alcohol campaigns) to educate and support non-opium consumption. In 1883 **Mei Quong Tart** presented a petition with 4,000 signatures to the government, effectively launching a crusade calling for a ban on opium imports.

Suffragettes

One of the earliest objectives of the movement was to gain equality amongst men and woman in Australia. The organisation began to be socially and politically accepted and legislated during the late 19th century, and was internationally instrumental in giving "the right to vote" for woman.

his Chinese roots and the land of his ancestors. In this age, not too many people remember Tart, but he would be an aspiration for any young people coming from China to Australia.

As he lived in the Sydney suburb of Ashfield, and being well respected, and loved, in 1998, Ashfield residents erected a statue of Tart. It is a bronze bust on a sandstone base, and organised by the West Regional Chinese people.

His children and descendants

Quong Tart had two sons and four daughters the last child being born just months before Quong's death. The children were: Vine (born 1887), Henrietta ('Ettie', b. 1890), Arthur (b.1892), Maggie (b. 1897), Florence (b. 1898), and George Henry Bruce (b. 1903).

Vine and Ettie both became nurses and Vine later worked in China in a governmental position.

Arthur was a wool classer but in 1907 enlisted in the Australian Army. This was in World War I. He suffered from shellshock and was gassed. He came back to Australia after the war but died in Brisbane in 1926.

Descendent – Josh Quong Tart became an actor.

Although it seems that most of Tart's descendants were well educated and did well in their various vocations, their life was not easy as there was still much racial tension and anti-Chinese sentiment.

Sam Poo Chinese bushranger

Sam Poo was a bushranger in New South Wales in 1865.

Poo, immigrated to Australia from China during the Gold Rush. Somewhat regarded as a "Chinese mystery man", a loner who mixed with neither whites nor Chinese. There were rumours that he had been a Chinese laundryman in Sydney, but on the gold fields he was nicknamed "Cranky Sam" due to his surly manner. One resident of Chinatown said, 'Him no good. Him bad man – no like.'

Portrait of Quong Tart, c.1880 – State Library NSW. Source: Wikimedia Commons

Quong Tart's monument (image kindly supplied by Anita Long)

Historical indicator for Sam Poo. (Permission granted Diane Simmonds of **www.mudgeehistory.com.au**)

Poo preferred the easier highway robbery than mining in central NSW. A skilled and elusive bushman, he evaded capture from the authorities for several weeks. He often targeted solitary travellers on foot, both Chinese and Whites, he did not care. He was also responsible for the **rape** of a settler's wife, keeping her with him all day and only letting her go at night, when he disappeared into the darkness.

At a lonely spot on the road, Sam Poo would rob at pistol point. At one time, he robbed two Chinese men of their hard earned gold dust that they had concealed under their pigtails in a calico pouch.

John Ward of the NSW Police Force was told that Sam Poo was in the vicinity in the bush. Following a short search, Ward located Poo's camp and crept up. When Poo saw the constable he ran into the bush. Ward chased him, during which a gun fight ensued, ending when Poo shot Ward in the chest. At the time it was reported that Poo said, 'You policeman, me fire.'

Poo took Ward's weapons before setting off into the bush. Ward lay helpless all day and night. However, about noon the next day the station (farm) owner, James Plunkett, who was riding by, found him. Trooper Ward gasped out what had occurred. Knowing that he was dying, Ward, in a shaky voice said, 'Take care of my wife and children'. He died shortly thereafter.

Citizens were concerned about Ward's family and collected money from the community around the area. This was presented to his wife.

A manhunt followed with armed and mounted posse-men. Aboriginal tracker, Harry Hughes volunteered his services and two weeks later Sam Poo was tracked down. When confronted by police troops he attempted to escape, and another running gunfight ensued, but this time Poo was shot in the thigh. Continuing to fire from the ground, the posse-men finally rushed him, but Harry Hughes, the Aboriginal, reached him first, where he clubbed the bushranger with his rifle butt, breaking the stock and fracturing Sam Poo's skull.

Sam Poo was taken to Mudgee, more dead than alive, to a prison hospital under guard. Nine months later he went to trial. Being found guilty of Trooper Ward's murder he was hanged at Bathurst Gaol on 19th December 1865.

Lew Goot-Chee and Wong Yue-Kung arrived in Melbourne in 1908 to raise support for the Chinese republican movement led by **Dr Sun Yat-Sen**. They co-edited the Chinese Times and gave lectures criticising the Qing (Manchu) dynasty. In an effort to counteract the influence of the monarchist movement in Australia, they formed the Young China League in 1911, with the New South Wales branch being headed by JA Chuey. The above came from the National Museum of Australia...

The thought of a Chinese Bushranger in Australia seems strange but in those early days of Australia, and because of the gold rush, all sorts of characters arrived. All in their own way helped to forge the character of current Australians. It is likely, that even if Sam Poo remained in China, his life would have ended up the same way.

***

The first Chinese-Australian River boat captain – John Egge

John Egge helped pioneer South Australia's lower Murray River area. Learning his trade under Captain Francis Cadell in the 1840s as a Chinese cabin boy to Captain, he sailed throughout the South China Seas. When Cadell returned to Australia and South Australia, be bought John Egge with him. After a time

Dr Sun Yat-Sen – Memorial outside the Chinese Museum Melbourne, in the heart of the Melbourne Chinatown

Egge took up his own command as a riverboat captain, and later became a merchant with his own store from the 1860s to the 1890s.

He became one of the wealthiest men in the Town of Wentworth, which is a little riverside town on the corner of NSW, Victoria and South Australia. A statue of Egge was erected on the wharf where he now happily gazes over the river that he spent so much of his life on.

***

The humble market gardener – "Georgie of Donald"

George Ah Ling (Lau San)**, (c1884-1987),** came to Victoria from Canton in a mail boat.

Before moving to the town of Donald in central Victoria, little was know of his life. Once in Donald, he became a part of the town – he became known as "Georgie of Donald".

For over fifty years, he grew vegetables in his garden using traditional Chinese methods. He would have woken up each day at dawn to work the fields, only stopping when it was too dark to see. He carried his two watering cans on a wooden yoke to water his vegetables from a nearby stream. Several times a week he sold his vegetables and fruit to the people of Donald, delivering them with his horse and cart.

Living in a simple shack, next to his garden, as his ancestors would have done for thousands of years. There was not much too his hut, I know because I saw it. In it, he would have had; a bed, a few tools in the corner, a chair and table, from which he would write letters to his family back in China. There may have been a photo or two of his family back "home", and possibly a shrine. Even though he had a simple life, he was a happy man, close to nature and all things natural. I wonder what he would think of modern China now – or modern Australia. He kept just enough money to survive, and keep his garden going, but sent most back to China for the education of his children, where apparently they became professional people in America – it would have taken many carrots and cabbages, all watered by hand, to pay for a child's medical or law degree.

George's happy nature and complete honesty endeared him to the people of Donald. It was said he was the only person who was welcome in every home. Members of the community helped him with food, and farmers brought feed for his horse and replaced it when necessary.

In his old age, his children wanted him to join them in the United States but Georgie said, 'Donald is my home'. On his passing, a plaque was placed at the site of his land.

(Some of the above was written in a short essay by Donald History and Natural History Group, 2013).

As I write this, I am in a town called Horsham, which is a bit over an hour's drive from Donald. I am here because my Winnebago is having repairs. So I drove my sedan (which I tow behind my "Winnie") over to Donald to see the plaque, and to see if I could "find" Georgie.

From the Sydney Morning Herald (NSW 16 Aug 1867)

William Bruce was indicted for what he did on the 9th July, 1866, near Braidwood, being armed, assault of one Kong Ah, a Chinaman, and rob him of one scarf pin, one saddle, and six papers.

The only evidence against the prisoner was that given by the prosecutor Kong Ah, a Chinaman, who being sworn in by the blowing out of a match, and interrogated through an interpreter, deposed that he was a gold-digger, and that on the evening of the 9th July, 1866, he left Braidwood for Jembaicumbene, and when he had reached a place known as the Big-Hill, about three miles from Braidwood, he was stopped by an armed man with black whiskers, and by the prisoner, who was also armed. Those men took him off the road, and while the prisoner searched him, the other man held a revolver to his head. They kept him in the bush for about half an hour, and then let him go. The witness swore positively to the prisoner's identity.

For the defence, a man named Roach was called who deposed, that he resided with his father on the Molonglo River, that he went to the prisoner's house on the 8th July, 1866, after two working bullocks, which, on the following day, the prisoner assisted him to drive for about four miles along the road – and that the prisoner's house was forty miles from Braidwood. This evidence tended to show that the prisoner could not have reached the place where Kong Ah was robbed on the evening of the 9th July. Constables Woodlands and Byrne were also called, and they proved that Tommy Clarke, the outlaw, lately executed, resembled the prisoner in face; that Pat Connell had large bushy black whiskers; and that at the period when Kong Ah was robbed Pat Connell and Tommy Clarke were in partnership.

Mr. DALLEY addressed the jury for the defence, the SOLICITOR-GENERAL replied, his HONOR summed up, and the jury, after deliberating for two hours and ten minutes, returned a verdict of "Not guilty."

There being another charge against the prisoner he was remanded.

Ah Lamb, Ah Fooh, Cong Hay, John Ah Yoke and Ah Cooee were also held prisoners by the bushranger gang.

From the above article, it looks to me like the process was manipulated.

Entering the town of Donald I was not all that inspired. It is a flat, wheat growing area, and being winter, it was just dreary and gray. The land also supports sheep but none could be seen. Although it was a Saturday morning, around noon, the little town was pretty sleepy with very few people about. Most of the shops were closed, but later I was assured that this being winter it is the slow period. To my mind though, after taking in the town, the fast period would also be the slow period.

The local museum was closed, and that was going to be my source of information, however the couple who managed one of the local motels was not only helpful, they were enthusiastically helpful. This couple, who were about forty-eight years of age remembered Georgie very well, and with fondness. With a big smile the wife reminisced about how all the kids wanted to ride on the back of Georgie's cart as it headed into town with produce. There was a kind of platform there for that purpose. When she was about seven, she and the other kids would run to catch up with the cart, and jump on that platform, believing they were being most secretive. Their little arms and hands would reach up to the tray and steal some of the fruit. They would not take much, just a piece or two to eat. Of course Georgie knew this, and apparently use to put fruit towards the back of the tray for the kids "to steel", whilst Georgie pretended to be none the wiser as he encouraged the horse along. The woman said he was a nice man who loved kids and was always smiling, and never known to shout at any of the children.

With their directions, I found Georgie's property (only an acre or two) and the plaque, about two and a half kilometres out of the town centre. After reading the plaque, and taking the photo, I straddled a barbed wire fence to get into Georgie's domain. The hut had collapsed with neglect – the couple said how sad it was that the historic society was not able to maintain it in a reasonable condition. Now, it was just broken brick, collapsed timber, and rusted iron. Nevertheless, it gave me a sense of the life Georgie lived.

I can only assume that since Georgie died, at 103 years of age, that the hut had seen no visitors, as there were many of his possessions scattered around. There was not much after seventy years of occupation.

As it happened, another shower of rain, accompanied with a cold wind, came whilst I sat amongst the roofless rubble, but this did not interrupted my contemplations of Georgie and his life.

Did I feel Georgie looking over my shoulder as I intruded his space? I cannot say I did, but I certainly know that I felt moved by seeing his meagre possessions, his humble way. Over on my right, in the dirt, lay an old boot. I wondered how many years he wore it. On the floor in front of me was a wide-brimmed hat that had been stuck to the floor for so long I had to peel it off the rough planking. This would have kept the hot sun off

Georgie's memorial

The following is *from; http://www.mudgeehistory.com.au/Chinese/Chinese_p1.html*

Gulgong differs in a business way from any goldfield town we have seen opened in this Colony since 1861, by reason of the enterprise exhibited by the Chinese Traders in competing with the Europeans. In Herbert Street there are 2 Chinese stores owned respectively by **Sun Tong Lee and Co***. and* **On Lee & Co***., which in size and stock compares very favorably with the European rivals. The site of the latter is the largest store under one roof on the goldfield, being 70ft l inch.*

his face, and the rain out of his eyes. There were a few dinted and rusting, enamel pots and pans laying on the floor, probably knocked over when the roof collapsed.

As I sat there, I remembered what the couple had said, that it was strange for them as children because Georgie was the only foreigner in town. After all those years of Georgie being there, he spoke virtually no English, yet he had friends, farmers who would call and sit with him.

Georgie, you sought after no possessions, and even though you had no family around you, you were a happy man – that for 103 years, you found happiness in the land, and in just being.

Renown Chinese herbalists Kwong Sue Duk (1853–1929) - the travelling herbalist.

Kwong Sue Duk became well known throughout Australia for his herbal remedies and ability to treat aliments such as: fevers, headaches, broken limbs, arthritic conditions and many more. At one stage he operated in Melbourne's (famous) Russell street.

Having been trained in China, Kwong Sue Duk first went to the Californian goldfields before coming to Australia, where he for a time settled and plied his talents in Darwin from his storefront.

Later though, he worked his way throughout the Northern Territory, Queensland, NSW and then Victoria, healing as he went. The records reflect that all who he came across him liked him for his kindness and generosity.

It was in Victoria where he was known as the 'Russell Street healing herbalist', helping the rich as well as the poor. Married four times and with twenty-three children, his legacy was well assured.

It does not matter with whom we talk in China, whether they love or hate their government, all are united in the love for their motherland.

From the book *The Global Game Changer* by Doris and John Neisbitt

Herbalists in Australia

From the earliest days of Australia, there were Chinese practitioners of Traditional Chinese Medicine (TCM). Locally, they were referred to as herbalists because of the use of herbs. Pretty much, all the herbs came from China. At first, their only clients were Chinese. The white people were wary of TCM and preferred Western medicine. After a time though, white people realised the benefits of TCM, especially when the Western medicine did not help their malady, where often the Chinese treatment was successful.

In Victoria (1925), legislation was to be lodged before parliament where only pharmaceutical companies or chemists could dispense herbs. However, the herbalists united and oppose the potential legislation and so it never came to being.

With the Second World War, and then struggles in China pre-1949, trade with China diminished, and with it the herbs – many of the older healers retired and were not replaced with younger healers. Over the last fifteen years or so there has been a resurgence and acceptance of TCM in Australia, to the point where even in every small town there is a qualified practitioner. Not all of these are of Chinese heritage, but many are.

Chinatowns

Just about every major town or city in Australia has a Chinatown. I well remember the first time I went to a Chinatown market. I was about fifteen and was enthralled with the exotic colours, people everywhere, looking at seemingly a million different products, and action everywhere. Vendors laughing, shouting, pushing and jostling for the best customers or the best orders, wheeling and dealing. You could buy every conceivable product and usually at a good price. But the food ... not to mention the flavours and aromas, all the different textures, some food eaten there and some to cook at home, spices by the dozens, improving flavour, that extra tang.

I still enjoy going to these markets and once I have wearied my legs from much standing and walking, I'll sit and watch the people; all sizes, shapes, colours and nationalities, some dark, some yellow, and of course white. Many chewing the food that they purchased, sauce drooling down their chin and onto their shirts, shopping bags weighing down their arms. Kids by the hundreds, also chewing, sweets and things as they run through the crowds, between legs, under tables, throwing things, and generally intent on having fun, irrespective of adults being there. The floors littered with papers and fruit peels, Coke tins, and all sorts. With every few meters, different aromas stimulate. Some strong, others weak and hardly perceptible – but they are there.

As I sit and watch and wonder about the people and what their lives are like and if they're happy. You see some are hurried, frowning as they have rushed in, bumping into people, to buy specific thing before heading back to their busy day. The visitors who enjoy themselves the most are the ones who go there with leisure on their minds. They are the ones smiling and laughing. Then of course, there are the vendors with trolleys and barrows to bring in more fruit or vegetables... "Scuse... scuse, out my way... please scuse," they shout. If summer, many are bare chested or have just a vest on. The trolleys are piled high with boxes of all sorts; television sets, pairs of shoes, chocolate, and fruits – you name it and those things are in those boxes, but not for long because soon they will be in some customer's car heading back to their suburb.

The last time I went to a Chinese market it was a big one in Sydney called Paddy's Market (see the photos). I was about to go to China on business and wanted to buy small koala bears to give as simple gifts, they are light and easy to carry, and the Chinese people love them. How ironic is it that I go to a Chinese market to

Welcoming lion at the entrance of the Sydney (Paddy's Market) Chinatown

The following is from the National Museum of Australia

Religion and joss-houses
Traditional Chinese religion, especially ancestor worship, was important in the lives of Chinese immigrants. Chinese temples or joss-houses were established in many goldfield towns and in cities. These joss-houses were dedicated to, and contained, the effigies of various Chinese gods and goddesses, including: Cai Shen (the God of Wealth), Guan Yin (the Goddess of Mercy), Guan Di (the God of Loyalty and protection from injustice) and Tian Hou (Goddess of the Sea), and Guan Gong (a third century warrior of the Three Kingdoms period; who was deified during the Song dynasty. He was adored because of his virtue, prosperity, loyalty and good fortune). (*Continued*)

(*Continued*)
Worshippers prayed and made sacrifices to their ancestors and these gods for health, prosperity, safety and good fortune.

Today, the best known joss-houses are the See Yup temple in South Melbourne, the See Yup temple in Glebe, Sydney, and the Temple of the Holy Triad at Breakfast Creek in Brisbane. There is also a reproduction temple in the Chinese camp at Sovereign Hill, Ballarat.

Many Chinese people in Australia also accepted Christianity in order to become part of the wider community. The Anglican, Wesleyan Methodist and the Presbyterian churches all established missions in the major Chinese centres. The Reverend Ernest Leong Gie (usually known as Leong On Tong) was one of the two leading Chinese Methodist ministers in Melbourne. The other was the Reverend James Lee Moy Ling. Cheok Hong Cheong, who was educated in Australia by Victorian Presbyterians, became the leading public voice of the Chinese in Australia and combined his Chinese community work with the leadership of the Anglican Chinese Mission in Victoria. This mission still operates in Little Bourke Street and the (*Continued*)

buy Australian koala bears that were manufactured in China, to take to China to give to my Chinese business associates and friends! If you meet any of my colleagues, please do not tell them that the koala bears that I bought came from China.

As I took in the atmosphere, I sipped tea, which could have been Green, or Oolong, Longjing, Tieguanyin or a thousand other flavours… As a kid growing up in Australia I used to be given tea to drink but I used to think that there was really only one tea until I went to China and learnt differently. At these markets, I would sit down and sample the ritual and different flavours. At Paddy's market that last time, I reflected on the folk-tale of how tea came about in China. It was some 5,000 years back when Emperor Shen Nung tasted what he thought was his boiling water. He was surprised and pleased as there was a pleasant taste. Upon looking, he saw that there were leaves from a wild bush that had apparently blown into his cup, and the water had turned a yellow-green colour. Therefore, tea became a refreshment. Tea-serving ceremonies with elegant tea ware were a symbol for wealth and status. I was also amazed to learn of the Tenfu Tea Museum that honours the Chinese tea-drinking traditions. I must go to this place when in China some time – perhaps you can take me?

Whilst talking about tea, let me tell you a story. Sadly, one that is true, but it is the way of the world. In the early days of the British being in China, they had an agreement with the Chinese authorities that they would not take the tea plants out of China. Of course, they did and set up tea plantations in India, and in what was then Ceylon, which is now Sri Lanka. This dishonesty was at the behest of the British Crown through The East India Company. The culprit was Robert Fortune, a Scottish botanist. This would have cost the Chinese government and people billions of pounds worth of revenue.

In the early days of Australia, Chinatowns developed within cities and bigger rural towns, with theatres, businesses, schools, of course shops and street market tables, and temples. Essentially, they gave a home experience to the Chinese in Australia. It offered continuity of their culture and heritage. Chinatown markets fostered benevolent societies, often based on clan or home district ties. Chinatown markets quickly developed across Australia to support the Chinese population.

As they developed their commercial and political structures, locally produced Chinese newspapers sprang up, disseminating information as well as reporting from China. As many were refugees who supported the Taiping Rebellion in China in the 1850s, they were keen to keep up to date of the happenings in China. Their anti-Qing dynasty attitude was a dominant influence on Chinese community life, which led to support for Sun Yatsen and the Chinese revolutionary movement, which overthrew, in 1911, the last Chinese emperor Pu Yi. There are numerous Chinatowns in Sydney. The Paddy's Market one I referred to is near the city, and

(Continued)
Chinese Methodist (now Uniting) Church in Little Bourke Street, Melbourne, is the oldest Chinese Christian building in Australia.

In New South Wales, the Reverend John Young Wai, originally an Anglican convert from Victoria, established two continuing Chinese Presbyterian churches in Sydney. The Reverend George Soo Hoo Ten, a Baptist convert from California, came to Australia and was ordained in 1886 at St Andrew's Cathedral. He extended the Church of England's mission in the Sydney Chinese community and through his work two churches were built, one in Botany and another in Wexford Street, Sydney. A few Chinese also attended churches of the Catholic and Baptist denominations.

Opening of the New Chinese Joss House, Emerald Hill, 1866 (wood engraving published in The Australian news for home readers). The Illustrated Australian News, 20 December 1866. 1750.0003.05, Chinese Museum Collection.

The Argus *(newspaper) reported* 1858 to 1865
Discussing the Chinese Joss-houses

Offering devout opportunities for worshipping according to the Buddhist rights, and deriving profit from the sale of incense sticks and other offerings.

The larger temples seem to be by association, whether as sources of gain we are unable to state. These places, at least in some cases, serve the double purpose of resorts for worship and of (the) courts for the administration of (Chinese) justice. Offences as committed amongst the Chinese are thus investigated before a tribunal, and a magistrate of their own selection, the latter receiving a regular and liberal salary. The punishments awarded from fines to corporal punishments.

The new Joss house was opened with a grand feast that lasted for nearly a week, and amidst an immense discharge of crackers. This temple is decorated inside and out with a lavish display of vermillion and gold and chintz. There was the waving of Dragon wing-shaped banners, bearing the inscription 'hung-ge haung' (temple of inflexible rectitude and fidelity), and the sound of Chinese music... During the day,

(Continued)

reckoned to be the biggest and best. But all are quaint. Just out of the main city, the Dixon Street entrance, on the northern side there are beautifully carved lions. Most people only give these a casual look as they come in. But like many things Chinese, great care was taken with these and for specific reason. Feng Shui experts were bought out from China to harmonise the market and the immediate area, thereby encouraging favourable Qi. And although, now, there are shoppers and visitors from all over the world, it was not always so, as there were opium dens and gambling, giving the area a less than salubrious feel. In those days no English was spoken – this was Chinatown.

(*Continued*)

hundreds of devoted presented themselves, and with prostrations, they presented their offerings on the altar of their deity. Gold and silver were scattered, and paper representing money was burnt, crackers were let off in tens of thousands.

Tea cup ceremony (image curtesy of Wikipedia Common)

Tea cup ceremony (image curtesy of Pixabay)

Entrance to Sydney's Chinatown

Hui-kuans (social clubs)

In the past, hui-kuans were a source of comfort to lonely Chinese workers or immigrants. They were in Australia, for one main reason – to earn money to send home (where home was still China). The clubs supported them socially and with news from home. They did more, such as raising funds to send a corps back home to his family or supported the aged or sick. They also collected funds to send home in the times of natural disasters in China.

For many, the clubs was the centre-hub of their life. The hui-kuans were also central to maintaining Chinese culture, organising Chinese festival. They had educational programmes so their Australian born children could maintain the culture and customs.

Today, the role of hui-kuans is not quite as strong because many Chinese-Australians regard Australia as home, and China as a strong influence on custom, culture and heritage, but they still do play an important role for Chinese communities.

The China Towns of today are situated where the early Chinese immigrants set up – with ramshackle tin sheds or shops, under a tree, out in the weather. Where at

(*Continued*)

(*Continued*)
first there was no formality other than a street that allowed pedestrians access, and of course a shopfront.

However, in the 1960s and 1970s the various town and city councils took a greater interest to ensure the informal trading area complied with standard ordinances. This was not their only reason; the councils wanted to support the Chinese community, business people, and residents alike, to have their own area. More so, the councils knew it bought in tourism, and tourism bought in money for the area and the council.

Yet, at the time, many of the Chinese community were wary of the council's motives. They thought it would be as a control, or to make China Town's like a zoo, where white people would come and gawk at the Chinese people. They wanted to be seen as normal Australians, and nothing more, and certainly nothing less. Currently all the reasons for those concerns have fallen away.

Even now, when one walks through a Chinatown many young Chinese people frequent them. Most of these young people are Chinese students studying in Australia. They come for the clothes, salons, and Chinese produced goods they cannot get in most shops and of course… the food!!

Lion - Sydney's Chinatown

In Sydney there is a suburb called Epping. It is a middle class suburb, where there are many amenities. Over the last twenty years, there have been so many Chinese people settle in the suburb it is now known as e-ping (as in eastern people in Epping).

Chinese New Year in Australia

Chinese-Australians celebrate the Chinese New Year, the same as the Chinese communities all over the world do. There is one major difference though. In China it is winter, and usually cold. Whereas in Australia, it is summer and usually hot. But other than the season, everything else of the tradition and culture are much the same as they have always been. Many of the Chinese people living in Australia return to China to be with family at this auspicious time, especially the students.

Like their family in China, it is an important time. One that represents time with family, good food, parades, dragons, firecrackers and noise, lots of noise, of shouting, drums, whistles, all in fun. The Australian versions are just as colourful, with bright signs and the colour red everywhere, beautifully designed traditional cloths, and of course the dragons. Good luck messages, verbal and written, are given with hope and interest. I am not so sure as to how many of the Chinese-Australian children know of the Nian monster. But still, fun is had by all.

One aspect that may be different is that Chinese-Australians may not be as devout, in kneeling or bowing to the ancestors as in China. The food, especially for the lunch, is traditional (that is if a family member has been trained to produce it in the traditional way). And, as far as I could see, the wishes of abundance, wealth, health and family are still offered.

Of course, it is the grandmothers and the elderly Chinese members of the family that try and keep the culture and traditions alive. But that applies for all the Chinese culture and tradition – it is the elderly who do their best to get the young involved.

The children stay up until after midnight, when the crackers start and go all night, with millions of white and red fire cracker paper colouring the road and paths.

The gold of the Bendigo attracted many Chinese seekers of wealth to the area. Even today, small quantities of gold are mined by the some of the still active mining companies, and individuals who work the rivers and land for nuggets (this as much for fun as for wealth). Once the alluvial gold had run out, some 2,000 Chinese remained and became respected citizens. Today there is a thriving Chinese community in the area. They are in every kind of vocation and business, and are well liked.

It is in Bendigo that the Golden Dragon Museum (and Guan Yin Temple) is situated. Opening its doors in 1990, for the reason of displaying and protecting the dragons, it is situated in Bendigo's Chinatown.

The museum makes several claims about two of it dragon exhibits. These are that in 1892, from Fat Shan on the Pearl River in China, the Chinese community purchased a sixty-metre long dragon (Loong). It has five claws (for royalty) and requires forty-six men for the legs, and five to carry the heavy head. The claim is that Loong is the oldest active dragon still in existence. However, because of Loong's age, in 1970, it was replaced by Sun Loong (New Dragon), which at 100 metres is claimed to be the largest dragon in existence. To parade Sun Loong, requires one person to carry the head (which is 29kg), three to carry the neck, fifty-two to carry the body, and one for the tail. It has 6,000 scales, 90,000 tiny mirrors, and 40,000 beads. Sun Loong, is lovingly carried by fourth and fifth generation Chinese, whose ancestors arrived in the goldfields of Bendigo. Most are members of the Bendigo Chinese Association.

A story told to me by one of the volunteers of the museum is that originally Sun Loong was the longest, but the Chinese people of Melbourne purchased a larger dragon. Therefore, the Bendigo community had Sun Loong's length increased to retain the status as the largest.

Loong (Circa 1892) (curtisy of Goldern Dragon Museum Bendigo)

Sun Loong (curtisy of Goldern Dragon Museum Bendigo)

Family structure

The structure of Chinese families in Australia varies, where occasionally (for newer arrivals) multi-generations share one household. This happened more in the earlier years but has been less frequent since the 1980s. The Chinese population follow simular patterns to the rest of Australians, where smaller family units live independently of other family households. It would seem that independence is enhanced through a strong earning power, where young family units can afford their independence. There is the exception where an elderly parent may live with their children and grandchildren, but this is often caused by the partner of the elderly parent having passed on.

The above is based on conversations with interviews I had.

From 1871 the Chinese community of Bendigo wanted to contribute to the Bendigo Easter Festival, and to represent the Chinese community. With the aid of local Chinese businesses and Chinese societies, they specially made traditional costumes (300 cases all together) from China. Apparently these costumes remained in service for close to 100 festivals (100 years), as well as other ceremonial occasions.

She is old, hard to tell how old. Her teeth are gone, just one or two left, standing like tombstones in a sparsely populated graveyard. She walks her grandchildren to schools, with a bent back, and a bit of a sway to help her along and relieve the pain from too much hard toil in her younger years. Still, the smile is there, the shine in the eyes, as the weathered face with its thousand crevices, lights up as she looks at the kids.

The clothes are old but clean, neatly ironed, and closer to traditional. Since coming from the old country in 1987, she has not worked in fields, for she now looks after the house and the grandchildren for her son and his wife Yena. She is happy. Why wouldn't she be? She is with her son and beloved grandchildren; whilst Yena is sweet and respectful.

She does all the cooking, washing, the cleaning, and although she does not speak English (she never had time to learn when she first arrived), she does most of the shopping. It is a busy life, but that is OK. She does get time to talk to old Mr. Chung up the road and have tea with Mrs. Xiong.

What makes her happy is her self-determined role to continue the culture, the food, the traditions, the respect – all are her job. Moreover, they are in this new land, and it is very different, but the "Chinese-way" will continue… must continue. Even her son and Yena sometimes forget, and so she has to give them a gentle reminder.

As she walks the children home from school, she talks to them in the old language, and she smiles. They chatter like birds, and every so often giggle at something that Nai Nai says.

The above story could be told about any one of the many thousands of Chinese-Australian grandmothers who support their multi-generational family.

Chinese Organised Crime in Australia

As this book is about Chinese-Australians, I only report on the Chinese Mafia, and or Triad societies that operate here, as opposed to all the other forms of organised crime. Australia, being recoganised as a wealthy country, has organised crime syndicates and gangs from many different countries.

It would seem to me that the Chinese gangs are no bigger or smaller, better or worse than the other organised crime gangs that operate here. All are insidious and play on the weaker side of humanity through drugs, prostitution, and worse, child prostitution, modern day slavery, sex-slaves, money laundering, credit card fraud and many other things.

The following is from the Australian Government website https://www.aph.gov.au/

> The attention of Australian law enforcement agencies has focused on Chinese organised criminal activity in relation to a wide range of matters, including drug importation and distribution, illegal gambling, illegal prostitution, extortion, immigration malpractice and money laundering. A relatively new area in which organised ethnic-Chinese are believed to be prominent in sophisticated credit card fraud. There appears to be no solid evidence of significant organised, ethnic-Chinese, street gang activity, although it is difficult to be sure as there are many media reports that refer simply to 'Asian' gangs.

> ... heroin arriving in Australia. The Report of the New South Wales Crime Commission... ... that 'the large importations mainly originate in China and South East Asia'... Australian law enforcement agencies believe that ethnic Chinese have been for many years, and still are, the major organisers of heroin imports into Australia... ...A report cited the National Crime Authority's Chinese liaison officer as saying that the Chinese had been linked to every major seizure of heroin in the previous two financial years... ... indicate the importation of heroin into Australia is well organised and dominated by Chinese Organised Crime groups. ... It is unusual to find persons of Chinese origin in a supply stratum involving small quantities.... is that the majority of the importation efforts of the Chinese criminal groups is geared towards supplying other, non-Chinese, groups for their own distribution networks. The Chinese operate what is largely a heroin wholesale business, with little evidence of their further involvement downstream into retail distribution... ... Modern triads trace their history to secret political societies formed in China during the 17th Century to overthrow the Ching Dynasty and to restore the Ming Dynasty to power... ...Triads today remain obsessively secretive and closed criminal fraternities.

Chinese escapees

The Chinese Government has embarked on a massive campaign against organised crime. The initiative, "people's war" extends to Australia where some Chinese Nationals of organised crime operate.

According to newspaper reports in March 2017, there are at least ten Chinese criminals hiding in Australia from the Chinese government. In the past, there has been cooperation between the Chinese and Australian Governments for extradition of Chinese criminals. Many are wanted on fraud and corruption charges from the Chinese government or Chinese businesses.

Australia and China are in discussions to sign a treaty for the formalised extradition of Chinese criminals from Australia to China.

One such alleged criminal is Hu Yuxing. According to Chinese media, Yuxing came from Taiyuan, Shanxi province and was the head of Taiyuan's housing reform office. The reports say that Yuxing managed billions of yuan for the social housing developments. However, the Chinese government alleges that millions have been "scooped" into personal investments to the value of some $71 million AUD, and therefore the Chinese authorities would like to interview Yuxing.

The Taiyuan Daily reported that Yuxing could "command the wind and rain" with his wide connections,

> **The Chinese Triads** have been linked to the creation and distribution of the deadly drug Ice, which has ravaged Australian young people in an "ice epidemic". The drug is quick to addiction and severely reduces brain functionality. Once damaged, there is no returning back to a healthy brain functionality.

and went on to suggest that Yuxing was "vermin". The report continued, "that when Yuxing fled to Australia (Perth), the people have been deeply hurt by the great and irreplaceable financial loss of housing funds."

My report here must say that Yuxing says that he is innocent and that he has been wronged. The Australian Government at this stage will not make a public statement on the Yuxing case but admitted that that they are working with the Chinese authorities on the matter.

***

The cooperation between Australian and Chinese law enforcement agencies have been successful in several large drug busts, from Chinese Nationals to Australia. Further to this, an article from *The Australian* said, "there are examples where Australia has been used as a safe haven for illicit Chinese funds, which have in turn been fed into the Australian property market". According to the current Australian Foreign Minister, Julie Bishop, "Australia would become a safe haven for Chinese criminals without an extradition treaty."

There has been some high profile Chinese criminals either detained or extradited. One such alleged criminal is Qi Guang Guo, who is believed by Law Enforcement NSW to be the leader of "Big Circle", an Asian criminal group.

According to NSW police statements, the Big Circle Gang practice extortion, prostitution, credit card fraud, violence, and drug importation. Big Circle is one the most influential of the crime syndicates operating in NSW and is connected to the Triads with their origins in China.

Reports continue, stating that seven of Guo's colleagues are now in prison. Guo, apparently came from Guangzhou City, China in 1988 on a six-month student visa, and has been here pretty much since then, apparently illegally. For twenty years, Guo has managed to avoid conviction for an illegal visa status and alleged crime syndicate charges. However, he is currently in detention and is likely to be deported.

Chinese-Australians - sporting prowess

Throughout this work, we have spoken of the intellect, medical mastery, bravery and determination of Chinese-Australian's – now we turn our attention to the sporting field. However, seldom these days can we talk about sport without including large companies in the discussion, promoting sport and making money out of sport. The same with Chinese Australian sporting ties. Sport is a lucrative market, and the big Chinese brands are evermore sponsoring teams in Australia to create awareness for their brands, such as Hauwei. Conversely, the large sporting clubs in Australia, which are run as business enterprises, want to take their brand and game to the massive Chinese market.

The positive though is that it does bring the two countries closer together with a business-to-business approach and sport to sport dynamic, which would be unlikely if the money was not there to back it.

In 2017, there was the first ever Australia-China Sports Summit, held in Shanghai. The Australian Minister for sport Greg Hunt, said, "The government recognises the power of sport to act as a bridge facilitating connectivity and promoting trade between the countries".

In attendance were representatives of many of the sports codes as well as some of the large Chinese companies, such as Gemba and Populous and the Australian Chamber of Commerce.

A memorandum of understanding was signed, with the aim of mutual support and collaboration on sports science.

The Australian Government, in Chapter Sixteen of the *Standing Committees on Foreign Affairs*, stated "relationships are an intrinsic part of the whole deal with China, but we need to get to know her and we need to look at her, not just as a superpower with geographic proximity to us and a big trade dollar. It has to be more than a marriage of convenience. We have to get to know the Chinese people so that relationships are built on trust, respect and transparency, and it has to come from both sides. It goes on to say that communication through culture and sport is a highly effective means of promoting understanding and awareness and bringing people together. It can have a flow on benefit for economic and political relationship."

It recognises that both sport and culture are a means to promote broader bilateral relationships.

Soccer

In soccer, there is more and more collaboration between China and Australia. For instance Australian soccer star Tim Cahill signed up and played for Shanghai Shenhua FC. The Shangai fans loved Cahill, and so the ambassadorial ship of Cahill playing in China was wonderful. Nevertheless, it was a mixed blessing for the Chinese when Cahill scored the two goals in Australia's 2 - 0 win over China in 2015. However, Cahill was unhappy after breaking his nose in a game for the Shanghai Shenhua against Guangzhou and the commentators laughed. Not sure if I would find that funny. However, this seems to be a trait of Chinese people, where you will laugh at a situation like this. We Australians would immediately be sorry for the pain/embarrassment caused, where you laugh at the way something unfolded. Once the funny side had been laughed out, then, there would be compassion for the plight of Tim Cahill – of which he may not have seen that.

Chinese football is improving all the time and the cooperation with Australia has helped that improvement, as Chinese stars are invited to play for the large Australian clubs.

We are also training Chinese kids as ball boys/girls.

Basketball

The two countries are playing more basketball internationals against each other. In fact, Australia Basketball signed an agreement with China's Golden Star International Investments for the purpose of cross-pollination of basketball.

Australian Rules Football (Aussie Rules for short, or simply, AFL)

This is very big in Australia, attracting 100,000 spectators at some games, not to mention the television audience. The League has set up an academy and sponsored the South China league. Also sponsored was a national Chinese AFL Rules football team, of which the first game had 7,000 spectators, and one being the Australian Prime Minister Malcolm Turnbull. There are now amateur clubs in many Chinese towns and cities. The players love the game but they do not have much of a following there. Perhaps in time.

In Australia, many Chinese-Australians like the game and so there are AFL Chinese language commentators and Chinese language websites.

Back in Australia, AFL has been instrumental in helping Chinese immigrants settle into the "Aussie way" of life.

Newspaper reports of the gold rush period said that the Chinese Australians were keen on Aussie Rules football. The first Chinese team to play Australian Rules was in 1899, in a hospital charity game for Melbourne's St Vincent Hospital. Annually, at least 80,000 Chinese tourists travel by tour bus to the goldfields of the Ballarat area (Tsin Chin Shan), and whilst there, they go to the ground to pay homage to that first game. It is now a part of the Australia sporting history.

There was one story in 1903 of Chinese-Australian John Hing, who beat up an opposition player after racial comments against his Chinese heritage.

More and more Chinese-Australians played the game with Chinese leagues, and Chinese Australian leagues. Even the White Australia policy did not stop the Chinese people from playing, such was their determination.

Cricket

As per Australian Rules, similar programmes are happening with cricket, where Chinese cricketers are hoping to qualify for the 2019 Cricket World Cup. Chinese players are often sponsored to train with Australian clubs. Sporting mandarins in China call cricket "the Noble Game" and plan to grow its popularity in China. They want to compete against other Asian cricketing nations. It was ten years ago that the first Chinese cricket umpires were trained, and are now growing the accreditation to instruct schools and universities.

A report from the Guardian newspaper (March 2015) gave a wonderful description of the place and the time of the gold rush.

Ballarat was split by a cultural fault line (of course this is a lovely analogy because most made their living underground in the goldmines of the area). English and Cantonese, the flutter of cards and the clacking of Mahjong tiles, whiskey and rice wine, opium and tobacco, Confucius and Jesus... ...For on this day they were united by the great Victorian game of Aussie Rules, which was to be the first Chinese Australian rules football game.

Australian Surf Life Savers in Shenzhen
The Surf Life Saving Association of Australia (SLS) has partnered with Shenzhen Surfing Association (SSA) to deliver lifeguard training programs for local volunteer lifeguards in the Shenzhen region, as part of an Australia-China Council-funded initiative.

Rugby

The Chinese military favour rugby and play a lot within their services. They are even now playing in the Olympic Games 7 Tournament.

Tennis

Australian Tennis are running more and more tournaments in China.

The Australian Open 2014 was won by Chinese tennis sensation Li Na.

I enjoyed her acceptance speech after beating Dominika Cibulkova in the final at Melbourne where she had the crowd in fits of laughter. After thanking her agent, she went on to say, 'Max… agent, make me rich… thanks a lot.'

Then to her husband, after facing him in the crowd, she said, 'My husband… now you're famous in China…' much laughter. 'Thanks to him with everything… travelling with me as my hitting partner… fixes my drinks, fixes my racquet… so thanks a lot,… you're a nice guy… also, you so lucky'. More laughter.

The Australians took to Li Na like she was one of their own. A great ambassador for China.

Swimming

Australian coaches has had great success helping top Chinese swimmers achieve gold at international tournaments, including the Olympics.

Kwok Chun Hang – a Chinese swimmer of 1935. A little known fact, although he was a swimming sensation in China, he was unknown in Australia.

In 1935 Kwok Chun Hang came to Australia and swam in the Australian National and Victorian Centenary Championships in Melbourne and won two breaststroke championships. Hang was the first Chinese swimmer to come to Australia to compete.

Hung's success created great media attention at the time here in Australia – not as much in China though, as they had their hands full with the Japanese invasion.

Other sports

Popular games in China such as badminton, table tennis and martial arts are also popular here, and our rankings are growing. Currently, we do not do very well on the world stage ... but watch this space.

I am not sure if the different forms of Qi Gong, such as Tai Chi, is regarded as a sport, but it certainly is gaining interest here, with people of all ages enjoying the activity. I for one, have been doing a Gong (Shenzen) for the last twenty odd years.

In Australia, more Chinese-Australians are playing golf, probably a game that they could not afford in China, or have the time. Golf is used as a social game but also has a business connotation as often business is done out on the course.

There is no doubt that sports bring countries closer together, fostering cultural exchange and understanding and I am interested to see the growing cultural and sporting pollination between our two countries.

The Arts

From Dfat.com.gov.au shows Society, Culture and Arts

Australia's links with China are led by our communities through education, cultural and artistic connections, but also through migration and tourism. Australian and Chinese familial, institutional and social networks are growing rapidly and further contribute to mutual understanding between our countries and people.

ACC goal: **Arts and Culture** – showcase Australian arts and creative industries to Chinese audiences and build closer and broader cultural and artistic partnerships (according to **http://cccsydney.org** on the 1st August 2015).

A Retrospective of Chinese Archibald Finalists

The Archibald Prize is awarded annually to the best portrait, "preferentially of some man or woman distinguished in art, letters, science or politics, painted by any artist resident in Australasia."

This unique exhibition celebrates the accomplishments achieved by Chinese artists in the Archibald Prize.

During the past two decades, twenty-three paintings from Chinese-born artists in Australia received high commendations for their excellence. A number of them were selected as finalists in the acclaimed Archibald Prize, among which some won the People's Choice Award. Others won the Holding Redlich People's Choice Award in the Salon des Refusés.

It is regarded as the most important portraiture prize in Australia, and has high regard internationally.

The exhibition highlights the artists' contribution to the multicultural dynamism of Australia and aims to inspire exchange of ideas and mutual understanding between Chinese and Australian artists.

"Chinese artists' unique style and perspective on Australian culture add an invaluable dimension to Australia's art scene, making a significant contribution to Australia's multicultural society."

Australia, the Australian Centre of Chinese Culture & Arts (ACCCA) is an international company specializing in Chinese culture and performing art entertainment shows.

OUR AIMS

The main aim of ACCCA is to introduce fine Chinese culture and performing arts to the mainstream of Australia as well as to provide top quality entertainment to the local Chinese community.

ACCCA would strive to promote and mix Chinese culture with other advanced culture trends and upgrade its status in the world culture market as well.

ACCCA will also endeavour to introduce fine Australia performing artists and musical troupes to China for performance and culture exchange.

OUR VISION

Creative, Spiritual, Artistic!

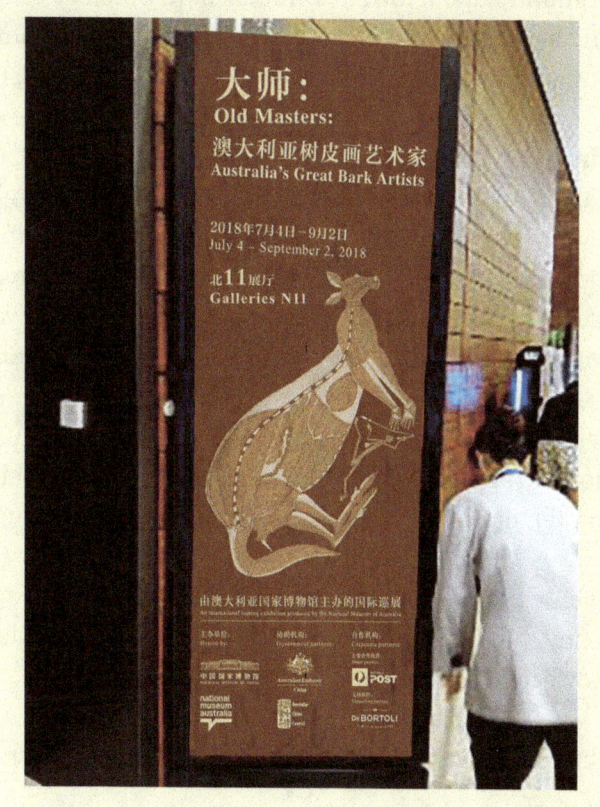

Edmund Capon, former Director of Art Gallery of New South Wales, expressed in his essay, "……the cultural and artistic horizons of the Western tradition of portrait painting have been enriched beyond expectation by our country's gregarious embrace of so many artists from China and our region."

Shen Jiawei was born in Shanghai in 1948 and became well known as a painter, not only in China, and Australia, but all over the world. Before arriving in Australia in 1989, he was popular with the Chinese government for his ‹revolutionary› images of the people, specifically the soldiers and workers of the period. Perhaps, his most famous piece was his, *Standing Guard for Our Great Motherland*, which he painted in 1974. Not only popular with the Chinese government and people, it was exhibited in the Guggenhein Museum in New York. His work was displayed in the National Art Gallery of China and the Museum of the Chinese Revolution in Beijing.

With medals, citations, and awards from within Australia and other parts of the world, his work is internationally applauded. Yet, Jiawei pretty much was self-taught. Later, with a full but varied method and subject matter, Jiawei produced large-scale history paintings.

Shen went on to paint many famous works of all subjects, but for a time settled on portraiture and painted many famous people including Crown Princess Mary of Denmark, the past Australian prime minister John Howard and many others.

Shen's wife Lan Wang is also a painter as well as sculptor.

Li Cunxin

Some of what I have written below comes from Li Cunxin's book, *Mao's last Dancer* (published by Penguin Viking, a wonderful read), as well as various websites, newspaper articles, and public domain. Li Cunxin is a superstar in many countries and so there is much information about him and his ballet exploits.

At twelve he was plucked from abject poverty, with no interest or knowledge in dance or any of the arts – how could he? Survival was ever present on his mind and that of his parents and siblings. Without enough food, running water, in minus fifteen degrees Celsius in the Shandong province of China, no shoes, and very little fuel to keep warm, life was impossibly difficult. Yet, the young Cunxin was selected to try out for what would become the ultimate prize, to train with Madame Mao's Beijing Dance Academy. At eleven, he had no concept of what was on offer, but somehow, his gut, his intuition, told him to grab it with all he had. His intelligence, talent and drive did the rest.

Cunxin wrote, "My family's earnings, as with all peasants, depended on the weather and luck… One year there was a severe drought and nobody was paid a single yuan for a whole year…despite our poverty, our parents always taught us to have dignity, honesty and pride."

The regime within the academy could have come from the dark ages, and was more designed for ancient warriors, where his body and mind were cajoled and pummeled into compliance. Buried deep, a tiny light ignited. This was in year three. It is hard to know if the light was love for dance or talent. Did the love of ballet nurture and develop the talent, or as the inherent talent emerged, love of the medium develop? Perhaps, one fed the other. It is likely to be both. The 10,000 or more hours of practice and tuition in that institution may have been sapping, but certainly, the young swan emerged from the ugly duckling.

At the Beijing academy, he also dared to try. It was there that he formed the wish to be one of the best dancers in the world, which he became.

Was it fate that selected the poverty-stricken urchin, with seemingly no ability or knowledge? Can fate be so grandiose, so orchestrated to be in such control? Or was it one of those trillion to one chances of his being in the right place at the right time? The way it reads in the book, is that it would seem to be more of the grandiose, because he was a last minute inclusion in the local trial in the Qingdao commune, almost as if, "OK, why not? You come." Then, like those spore that washed up on a beach to form humankind, against all odds, the peasant Cunxin somehow scraped through each level of elimination, each round of adjudication, and at each time with seemingly nothing to offer. It was only in his third year at the academy that one of his masters saw that fledgling flame, and was able to fan it. Perhaps his mother said it best. 'There is a God who has looked after you and steered the course of your life.'

Cunxin fell in love with Mary McKendry, also a leading ballet dancer. Mary is Australian, and so after sixteen years at Houston Ballet, Cunxin, he and his young family moved to Melbourne Australia to perform with Australian Ballet and became a principle performer there. Later, he became the Artistic Director of the Queensland Ballet, and had many successful years developing that institution to one that is recognised.

What I loved the most was his obvious gentleness and compassion. This, like the tide coming in, quietly extended to his immediate family (seven brothers), his neighbours, then the people within his sphere of influence as he became better known. The other thing that struck me was his love for China, and the people of his home country. The man may have left China, but China never left him. Now, his children are likely to continue the link between the two countries, as they are fluent in the language.

Some of the accolades he received

Three medals for the three international ballet (world championships) competitions he entered.

Named Queensland's Australian of the Year in 2013, and later, narrowly missed out on being awarded Australian of the Year.

- Wrote the bestselling book, *Mao's Last Dancer*

When he performed in Beijing in 1979, the Central TV of China broadcast the event live to an audience 500,000,000 in Chinese

He was asked to perform at all the premier events worldwide.

A tribute given in the aforementioned book (by Leanne Benjamin, Principle Dancer, Royal Ballet), "Anyone who has a burning desire to reach great heights should read this book."

In 2009 he was named the Australian Father of the Year.

And if that is not enough, the Queensland Museum named a species of spider (that had recently been discovered) after him. The spider, apparently, has a beautiful mating dance.

However, his story does not end there, after eighteen years away from the dancefloor, too many years, Cruxin is returning to perform one last time. He is once again stressing and straining his body, but this time, not the young reed-like body that could bend double in youth. This is an older body, with bone and cartridge more wooden, solid and inflexible with age, where ligaments and muscles are asked to do the impossible.

At the time of this writing, we have not been blessed with Cunxin's return performance, but I, like many millions wait with anticipation.

But who is he now? Australian, Chinese or American, perhaps he is the best of all of them.

The last thing about this amazing man – his teacher and mentor from his days at the Beijing academy said this to Cunxin, "You did Chinese ballet proud."

Recognising Chinese Tourists in Australia

The Australian Federal Government, and the various State Governments, recognise the value of Chinese Tourists. Hence, there are signs in Chinese to help the tourists. These are in railway and bus stations, and most tourist destinations.

One the opposite pages are a selection of these.

Australian signs, in Chinese

Of Chinese Driving or Drivers in Australia

Over the last few years there has been much coverage in the Australian press of bad driving or dangerous driving by Chinese tourists in Australia. It seems that every few weeks there is another story. Even at dinner parties, often the Chinese tourists driving comes up for discussion – and it does seem to be the tourists and not the residents who drive badly.

I was chatting to a friend the other day and she told me that she had to go to the panel beater the next day to have her driver's side wing mirror fixed. She went on to tell me that she had been traveling a busy one-land (each way) rural road at dusk the previous Sunday, when suddenly a car started to overtake her, but so close did that car pass her, that it "took out" her driver's side mirror. At first my friend was too shocked to do anything, but then anger took over and she took after the driver. As the driver kept speeding and overtaking other cars, so did my friend to keep up. This went on for about fifteen minutes until finally the errant driver pulled over to see why this car was flashing and honking its horn all the time. As my friend pulled over behind that car, another car pulled over behind her. It would seem that the car behind my friend had a dash camera, which recorded the original incident and so he kept up with the chase because he thought his footage would help to support what happened.

As people from the front car got out of their hire car, it was clear that they were Chinese tourists. One of the passengers spoke a little English, very little. When my friend showed them her side mirror, they were shocked (although, I cannot see how they did not know that they had done this). When my friend went and looked at their passenger mirror, it was also smashed. The Chinese were very apologetic and to try to help – the driver put his hand in his pocket, brought out a bunch of Australian dollars, and started to pass them to my friend as way of payment. My friend though was not willing to do it that way and felt it needed to be done the correct way, through insurance and so did not accept the money. The Chinese driver did accept responsibility... well he had to as it was all on camera.

When I started this piece, I said that there are numerous stories about poor driving from Chinese tourists. I have a theory on this, and it goes to suggest that in a lot of the cities of China, people do not get experience of open road driving, or driving at high speeds as there is just too much traffic. When they come to Australia, they literally have to "learn" on the roads.

Here is an article from around about 150 years ago.

The Argus, 15 November 1861 wrote the following:

We learn from our Creswick correspondence that, as the Chinese coach for Castlemaine was turning the corner by the bridge over the creek at Creswick, on Tuesday last, the Chinaman driving allowed the horses to run on the embankment, and thereby capsized the coach. Two passengers were injured severely – one having his arm and the other his leg broken. To judge, says our correspondent, by the style of driving exhibited here almost daily by the Chinese drivers, they are a very incompetent lot, not fit to be entrusted with the lives of human beings.

It would seem that the Chinese got off to a bad start here.

However, I shudder at the thought of getting behind the wheel of a car in China, where the wheel is on the left side of the car (not the right side as here in Australia), then driving in that Beijing or Shanghai traffic, also on what would be the wrong side of the road for me. I nearly get killed as a foot pedestrian when crossing the road thinking the oncoming traffic should be on one lane only for it rush at me from the other. So for Chinese tourists coming here would be equally difficult.

For non-Chinese readers

In Beijing, there are so many people wanting to drive, yet the roads are already clogged, the pollution... well. To limit the number of cars on the roads there is a lottery. One in nineteen are lucky enough to get that registration.

But I do note with interest that there is one article that said the Chinese authorities in Beijing recognise that there is a lot of bad driving in that city, and that they have set out to try and better educate the drivers, for not only safer driving but also for courteous driving.

Another article suggested that internationally, Australian drivers are recognised as not being good drivers, for instance they are lazy when it comes to using their indicators and a lot of their driving just seems to be lazy or slovenly. I have no doubt that Chinese-Australians, after they have been here for a while, are as good as anyone on the roads. The one article made the suggestion that before Chinese tourists start driving here that they complete a driving test to prove competency. That is probably a good idea but to my way of thinking, it probably would be a more bureaucratic way to make more money from international tourists.

Another article that I read from an English language Chinese report made the point that a high percentage of the drivers licenses that have been issued in Beijing have been issued within the last ten years. This means that in China there are many new drivers. It went on to say that ten years ago cars were not as available to the population as they are now, and so with the explosion of cars in China there is an explosion of new licenses too. In Australia, it is well known that most of the accidents that happen here are from young and inexperienced drivers. Therefore, to be a competent driver does take a bit of time on the road.

The worst drivers I have experienced are the drivers in South Africa who drive the commuter taxis. They think nothing of running down pedestrians on the pedestrian footpath as they hurtle along one to avoid traffic at a traffic light, or to overtake some slow driver. I lived in South Africa for many years and so was aware of the scary driving and the broken cars that are on the road. I remember reading one article where one of those same commuter taxis had killed a pedestrian because the brakes did not stop the car. Upon investigation, it was seen that the driver had inserted cardboard to replace the worn out brake pads. After all, cardboard is cheaper than proper brake pads!!

Chinese Investment in Australia

Chinese-Australians have been an integral component of the commercial landscape of Australia. It is driven from two sources: Chinese-Australians within the country and large investments directly from Chinese companies and individuals from mainland China. This is especially so over the last thirty years. It does go further though, as Australia does a lot of business in China, as the following report reflects.

On 17 July 2015, the news website **http://www.news.com.au** announced a new trade deal with China, marking a new future for the two nations. "The unprecedented agreement that we have signed today will not only enhance trade between our nations but also two-way investment," Mr. Abbott (the Australian Prime Minister of the time) said. "It will change our countries for the better, it will change our region for the better, it will change our world for the better."

The historic trade deal will mean Australian beef and wine can be more readily exported into China. He said more than just investment, the deal was about the growing trust between the two nations. "Our investment … it's proof of our trust in China," Mr. Abbott said. The agreement will make it cheaper for Chinese consumers to buy goods such as Aussie beef, dairy, wine, boutique whisky, sea cucumbers, opal products and even deer velvet, by reducing tariffs on those products by up to 95 per cent.

Further to this, Australia is a member of the Chinese initiative for the Asian Infrastructure Investment Bank (AIIB), which aims to support the building of the **Asia-Pacific** region. The bank opened its doors on the 25th December 2016.

The South China Morning Post, wrote on the 19th April 2018 (only yesterday):

> The Asian Infrastructure Investment Bank (AIIB) is a China-led international financial institution created to offer finance to infrastructure projects as part of China's Silk Road initiative, with a focus on bolstering links across Asia, the Middle East, Africa and Europe. Some government officials and analysts have said growing dissatisfaction among emerging economies at the failure to reform the International Monetary Fund's decision-making system encouraged China to set up the new international lender, with 57 participating countries.

I see AIIB as a much-needed competitor to the World Bank, which to my mind has often fallen short of its manifesto. I also think competition to any standing organisation is good for all on the planet.

It has been this way for a long time.

From the National Museum of Australia

Chinese traders established lucrative markets for bananas in Sydney, Melbourne and many country towns, and some expanded their enterprises by establishing banana plantations in Fiji. These Chinese merchants were highly regarded by the European community for their excellent business sense and reputation for honesty. Three such merchants were **Mei Quong Tart** in Sydney, Lowe Kong Meng and Louis Ah Mouy in Melbourne. Chinese traders dominated the banana market until the First World War. Today, they still retain about 10 percent of the banana trade.

Also from the National Museum of Australia

Between 1900 and 1914 a large number of Chinese people in eastern Australia were primary producers. Market gardens were concentrated in and around the cities of Sydney, Melbourne, Cairns and Perth. In 1901, there were 799 Chinese storekeepers in New South Wales, more than half of whom operated in the Sydney area, usually as greengrocers. Chinese market gardens provided a comfortable return to their owner-operators for the investment of hard work and knowledge attained over thousands of years.

The Nomchong family is an institution in Braidwood (near Canberra), New South Wales. For a hundred years they ran a very successful general goods business serving the local community and the region around them.

The China–Australia Mail Steamship Line

The year 1914 was horrendous as the war, which was considered "the great war" was in full swing. This however did give opportunities to those with insight. With all the Australian and British (as well as the enemy of the time, Germany), ships being used for the war effort in Europe, this meant there was a shortage of ships working the Australia to Hong Kong route. However, Japan was one country that had ships working the route, and without competition, they saw fit to increase their tariffs.

In stepped the Sydney Chinese Chamber of Commerce, which included William Liu, Ping Nam, William Gockson and Thomas who helped establish the China–Australia Mail Steamship Line.

January, 2018 saw the release of the Migrants Small Business report which reported 80% of the immigrants to Australia start their own business. This shows the immense contribution that immigrants make to Australia – currently employing 1.4 million people, where they specifically upgrade and upskill the younger Australians. The report said that the immigrants who started their own enterprise were even across all migrant nationalities.

I have a 4.5 year old grand daughter, and when she heard I was going to China, she asked, 'Granddad, when you come back from "Made In China" will you come and visit me?'

China buys more wine from Australia than any other country.

According to News.com.au (January 2018), Australia is the second favourite offshore investment destination for Chinese buyers, behind the United States...

The Chinese Hawker, **wood engraving c1873. 1985.07.29, Chinese Museum Collection.**

Excuse the pun, but it was not always "smooth sailing" for the company. The two ships they purchased were quickly commandeered by the Australian government for war service. Thereafter, there were many difficulties, such as the raising of enough capital, and then after the war the return of the pre-war shipping lines as strong competition.

Around 1947, there was a decline in the number of Chinese-born in Australia, which dropped from around 29,000 to 6,000. However, those who remained in Australia saw vast opportunity and started many forms of business. To support each other and the Chinese community, different organisations, such as the *See Yap Society were* established. These societies were benevolent but often supported members from their home region in China. The See Yap Society still exists and is one of the oldest continuing organisations in Australia, where they have chapters throughout the main centres of Victoria.

As mentioned above, land ownership within Australia is likely to be a large consideration to the Australian economy, with more international buyers scrambling for Australian space. Most prominent of these international buyers will be from China.

There are two main areas of foreign land ownership. One is for agricultural holdings, as foreign countries want to secure a "food basket" for their own populous. The other is inner city real estate for major investments.

There are some in Australia who rebel against China being such a prominent purchaser of Australian land, suggesting that "they" will buy it all. Because of this, the Australian Government called for a report on foreign land ownership in Australia. This reflected that Chinese investors have a very small percentage of Australian land, and are behind The United Kingdom, United States, Netherlands and Singapore in Australian holdings. Once the report, as created by the Australian Tax Office, was released, reflecting that China consortiums only have 0.4% of total landmass, or 2.8% of foreign-owned holdings, xenophobia over China's supposed dominance relaxed.

Nevertheless, Chinese companies do have massive shareholdings in numerous agricultural ventures, and are always seeking more. They are also active in buying inner city holdings in all the major cities of the country.

Further to this, China is Australia's largest growing trading country, and is likely to continue to be so for many years into the future. This would mean that the ties between our two countries, both socially and business wise, is likely to grow.

On Chinese honesty

In the 1870s, twice there were placements in the Advertiser of Central NSW by Sun Ton Lee, a Chinese trader. The first was that a purse had been found with money. Sun Tong Lee had printed that if not claimed within 14 days the purse would be given to the Treasurer of the Gulgong Hospital.

Then in 1873 another purse was found and a notice given. The thankful owner of the purse offered his gratitude in another placement. *I wish to advise that I have received from Sun Tong Lee, the amount of thirty six pounds five shillings being the amount in the purse he found, which belonged to me. It is much appreciated for the trouble he went to* Signed G. R. BROWNE, Gulgong.

Thirty six pounds and five shillings would have been a large amount in those days, perhaps the equivalent of $20,000 in today's money.

Ma Ying-piu was born in 1864 and was from Heungshan, Kwangtung. At eighteen years of age, he sailed to Australia where he established the Wing Sang Co., Ltd in Sydney. Although the business did well, he wanted to return to China. Upon doing so, he opened what is believed to be the first department store in China called the Sincere Co, Ltd. Success was assured and it had branches in Shanghai, Canton, Singapore and Namning.

Kwok Bew, born in 1868 near Canton, China, became an influential businessman mogul in Australia and China with Wing Sang & Co. In 1883 he left China and came to NSW. At first he worked as a door-to-door salesman – imagine how difficult this would have been with only newly-learnt and broken English? Later, he changed vocations to become a produce merchant in Sydney.

In time he was to become known as George Bew. In 1896, George married Darling Young, in the Presbyterian Chinese Church in Sydney. Young was a daughter of a Bourke merchant.

Over time, the company of Wing Sang & Co. expanded from general produce into a fruit and vegetable agency. His suppliers were Chinese gardeners in Northern NSW, Queensland and the Pacific region. The company expanded and was soon to control most of the wholesale banana market in Australia.

Bew emerged as a Chinese business leader of great influence. One venture was that he was one of the main investors in the formation of the China-Australia Mail Steamship Line in 1917.

Always an advocate for Chinese commerce in Australia, Bew was active as the vice-president of the Chinese Merchants' Defence Association. This association was created to fight the propaganda and miss-information of the 'White Australia' merchants. He was also involved in the establishing of the *Chinese Republic News* in Sydney. This newspaper was widely circulated throughout Australia, even into the South Pacific, Hong Kong and China.

In 1917 he returned to China and founded the Wing On Emporium in Shanghai. The Emporium became one of the largest department stores in China.

Next, in 1920 he moved into the lucrative banking industry, then manufacturing, and even became a director of the Chinese Government Mint.

Bew died in 1932

William Joseph Lumb Liu was born in 1893 in Australia to his Chinese born father and English mother. William, at seven years of age, went to stay in his father's village in Taishan county, Guangdong province, China, for eight years.

After returning and finishing his education, he had various jobs (as he seemingly, groomed himself for the very top) until he
(Continued)

(*Continued*)
joined Wing Sang & Co., and was part of that management team for thirty odd years. He was also a member of the team that started the China–Australia Mail Steamship Line, and for a time was the general manager.

In 1916 he married Mabel Ting Quoy.

Lui became president of the Kuomintang in Sydney, where in 1921 he meet the Chinese leader, Dr Sun Yat-Sen in Guangzhou. In addition, as Vice President of the NSW Chinese Chamber of Commerce, he was instrumental in convincing the Australian government to appoint an Australian trade commissioner to Shanghai in 1935.

A vehement opponent of Japanese imperialism, in 1931 Liu compiled the book *China and the Trouble in Manchuria*, condemning the Tanaka memorandum. In 1932, he was living in Shanghai when the Japanese invaded. Behind the scenes, and risking his life, he worked as a propagandist for China's 19th Route Army.

During World War II, Liu was tireless in lobbying the Australian Government for funds for the Chinese community. He was also supportive towards the Aboriginal people of Australia.

In 1981 Liu received an OBE (a Queen's Honour) for the giving of services to the public.

Figures released in March 2017 show that property remains a popular investment for Chinese millionaires. Chinese investment accounts for almost 80 per cent of all foreign housing demand in New South Wales and Victoria.

Although the following was written some five years ago it reflects the financial power of China and Chinese business people to enter international markets.

During the next five years China will account for nearly five percent of the increase in emerging economies wealth (Credit Suisse Global Wealth report 2013). Urbanization and the strategic planning of urban economic clusters have supported its growth. Many Chinese cities have higher GDPs than some countries in the world.

From *The Global Game Changer by Doris and John Naisbitt*

The Chinese Contribution to Australia

How does one measure the contribution to a country from a sector of its immigrants, and in this instance people from China? Of course, there is the investment contribution, which is important, and we will talk a bit more about this in a minute. However, to me, the most important contribution would be that as measured by sociologists (someone who studies society and social behaviour by examining the cultures and society groupings). Although it was suggested that I write this book, it really is a compilation of the sociological effect on the Chinese-Australians on this country – and so I am sure that once you have finished the book, you will have a good understanding of the Chinese contribution to Australia. You will have seen the contribution of the Chinese people in helping to build this wonderful nation. How is that measured? What about their art? Or the mouth-watering Chinese cuisine that tantalise our taste buds and gets our gastric juices pumping.

Now, back to the investment contribution aspect. Economists have all sorts of tools that measure the financial contribution to an economy from a specific grouping. Some are likely to measure direct investment, and others measure the earnings from Chinese Australians that was re-distributed back into the Australian economy. Chinese-Australians have proven to be wonderful entrepreneurs, and as reported earlier a few pages back, a high ratio of Chinese men and women have started their own companies here. Their import and export business has been a boon to this economy.

Certainly, the investment effect on this country in the past is probably small beans compared with the current and future investment coming from the China mainland. How will that shape Australia?

Having said that, even though Australia has been heralded as the most successful multi-nation country in the world – on the 11th April 2018, the Human Rights Commission announced that even though roughly 25% of the population were not born here, only 3% are accepted as top CEOs of Australian companies. So what does that say about the entrenched physic of the country? Well, the Human Rights Commission went on to say that our egalitarian nature is not as strong as it should be, that our success as a multi-cultural nation still has a long way to go. We should be aiming for a more cultural diversity in our business leadership in our institutions.

From the Australian China Council website

ACC and Australia-China Business Council (NSW) are partners in the new project to further expand collaborations between Australia and China on food security. Food security will be one of the most critical issues of this century. Australia and China have a considerable track-record in working together on agricultural and food security projects. There are numerous opportunities to grow our cooperation through joint research, two-way investment and commercialisation. The China-Australia Food Security Initiative (CAFSCI) aims to become a leading platform for collaboration and information exchange between Australian and Chinese researchers, agencies and agribusinesses. One of the main elements of the project is a comprehensive database of joint agricultural research and commercialisation projects and Australian agricultural technologies... CAFSCI.

True knowledge is when one knows the limitations of one's knowledge.
Confucius

Who really discovered Australia?

In 1770, Captain James Cook of the British Royal Navy was thought to have discovered Australia. And when landing on shore, he placed the Union Jack (the British flag) firmly into the ground. And although Cook may have claimed Australia for the British Crown, it has become known that he was not the first to arrive on those shores. *The Age*, a prominent Australian newspaper, on the 25th November 2002, carried the headline, "It's official; Admiral Zheng beat Cook to Australia." The article goes on to say, that there is much academic debate over the suggestion that China's Admiral Zheng, in the 15th century, with his fleet of colossal nine-master teak junks, were here much earlier. Some 350 years earlier.

His main reason for coming to and exploring Australia was for mineral exportation, and to that end, they set up camps in Australia. However, Zheng's great supporter, the Emperor Zhu Di, was overthrown by his son Zhu Gaozhi, who ordered that there be no more exploration of the area. Therefore, that was that.

For now, the argument continues to rage as to who first discovered Australia, but imagine if Zhu Gaozhi did not stop the

(Continued)

The anatomy of a body is made up of roughly fifty trillion cells, which all contribute to the overall good. It would be difficult for any researcher to be able to say that this person's personality is like it is because of XYZ cell. Therefore, it is with the anatomy of Australia. The Australian character and the uniqueness of the Australian culture is as a result of the collective cultures of the country.

What follows are biographies of just some of the Chinese immigrants that made a big difference to Australian culture.

Bill O'Chee was known to be unconventional. He became an Australian parliamentarian at only twenty-four years of age. He the first Australian senator with Chinese ancestry. O'Chee's father (William) was Chinese-born and his grandfather Lau Oh Gee first came to Australia in the 1930s with William. Later, the name Lau Oh Gee was mistakenly written O'Chee by an immigration official. Despite the love of his homeland, William forbid Bill from speaking Cantonese and forced him to speak English. So well did Bill learn how to speak and pronounce English, he won an interschool's public speaking competition and at only twenty-one, he competed in world championship debating.

As a youngster, Bill was interested in politics and became a member of the Young Nationals.

He was awarded a scholarship to attend secondary schooling in England. Thereafter, he attended Oxford University, where he read Jurisprudence (the theory or philosophy of law), graduating with BA Hons in 1987. As a senator, Bill was a champion for many causes, such as the economic situation of the poor, environmental issues and even youth issues. Always the advocate for Chinese-Australians, he remembered racism against him as a child – things like 'ching chong Chinaman' and 'two wongs don't make a white'. He also supported advances for the First Nations people of Australia. He did not like the term multiculturalism and felt that all the cultures make this nation.

Although recoganising himself as fully Australian, Bill O'Chee always acknowledged his Chinese ancestry.

(See the speech by Bill O'Chee below)

William (Bill) Ah Ket was of Chinese heritage and was born on in 1876 in **Victoria** Australia, from parents Mah Ket and Hing Ung, both from China. Well educated, and clever, Bill did law at University, and later developed into a barrister of note.

(*Continued*)
exploration and had it continued – what then? What contribution would the Chinese have made to this land?

Two last comments on this. That the First Nation's people of this country would dispute that they needed to be "discovered".

The second is about Captain James Cook. Irrespective of him "discovering" Australia or not, I think that he will go down in history as the greatest Explorer that ever trod the earth or sailed the seas. His achievements were extraordinary.

From The Global Game Changer by Doris and John Naisbitt
More than 80 percent of the world's population is in the process of nation building, learning from the advances and mistakes the West made. In *Mind Set!* they wrote that in China the periphery is the center. What was true for China is now true for the world. What once was pictured the periphery of the West, the countries of Asia, Africa and Latin America, are transforming to new economic centers in a multi-centric world.

Images of the Endeavour Replica (this is a real working model that is used for training, and historical exploration).

As a champion for the downtrodden, and especially the Chinese-poor, he fought for the Chinese to overcome the difficulties of the 1907 *Factories* Act. With success, Bill improved the conditions for many of the Chinese workers.

Later, he co-founded the Australian-Chinese Association, and in 1912 was a delegate, representing the Chinese community from Australia at the opening of the Chinese National Parliament. From the years 1913 to 1917, he was the Consul-General for China in Melbourne.

John Ian Wing was born 1939 in Australia of Chinese descent. For many years John and his family lived in a unit above his father's Chinese café in downtown Melbourne.

In 1956, Melbourne Australia hosted the Olympic Games. At seventeen years of age, Wing conceived an idea to foster goodwill amongst the international competitors and the public. Wing wrote a letter to the **International Olympic Committee** suggesting that the athletes from all countries circulate together at the closing parade as a symbol of global unity. This suggestion was approved and is now Olympic tradition. Apparently, Melbourne was dubbed the "Friendly Games" because of this.

However, when Wing wrote the letter, he did so anonymously as he felt embarrassed that he was bringing shame on his family by being upfront to "important committee" people. He also did not want to look foolish if the suggestion was scoffed at.

But many years later, and with continued interest in this, Wing wrote a second letter to the committee informing them that he had written the first letter and that the suggestion was his. He stated his reasons for his anonymity. He was duly recognised for the suggestion, and was thereby honoured with an Olympic medal for his contribution of global unity. And now, a street at the site of the Sydney Olympics (2000) bears the name John Ian Wing Parade in his honour.

Dr Victor Chang (cardiac and transplantation surgeon) was a pioneer of the modern era of heart transplantation and was responsible for setting up the National Heart Transplant unit at St Vincent's Hospital in Sydney in 1984.

Sadly, Dr Chang died in 1991 from two bullets to the head in a botched extortion. Chang's death resulted in a national outpouring of rage, shock and grief for this dedicated and compassionate man.

Born in 1936 in Shanghai, China, as Chang Yam Him, Chang, along with his sister came to Australia in 1951. Staying with his Aunty Fung. Finishing his school in Sydney, he then studied medicine. A brilliant scholar, he was awarded a Commonwealth scholarship whereby he spent a year doing research before graduating in 1963. He continued his studies (for a time in England) to qualify as a fellow of the Royal College of Surgeons of England. Further studies took him to the United States before returning to Australia.

In 1984, The National Heart Transplant Program for Australia was conducted at St Vincent's Hospital, Sydney. As head of that department, Chang conducted 266 heart transplants – and was recognised as one of the leading heart transplant specialists in the world. He also performed twenty-two heart-lung transplants, as well as developing a heart valve which now is used all over the world.

Not only that, he was instrumental in exchanges of medical personnel in hospitals in South East Asia. After the development of the heart valve, he ensured that they went to third world countries at reduced costs.

Other accolades:

- at the time of his death, Dr Chang was working on an artificial heart.
- appointed honorary professor of surgery to the Chinese Academy of Medical Science in Beijing and at the Shanghai Medical School

John Ian Wing Parade

- appointed to the Australia-China Council, whereby he helped influence rapport between Australia and Asian countries
- received a doctorate of medicine honoris causa from The University of New South Wales
- was voted Australian of the Century at the People's Choice awards in 1999
- a recipient of the Order of Australia Medal (Companion of the Order of Australia)
- known for his humanitarian work

A state funeral service was conducted many thousands mourned him.

Helen Quach (Kuo Mei-Chen) of Sydney, won first prize in the New York Dimitri Mitropoulos International Competition for Conductors in 1969.

Professor Christopher Chen became a recognized world pioneer in in-vitro fertilisation (IVF). In 1982 he succeeded in producing the first IVF pregnancy in South Australia and, a year later made history by presiding over the birth of the world's first IVF triplets.

In 2012, Professor Chen gave a donation of $10.5 million to The University of Queensland to further his research. The gift is one of the biggest individual donations the university has received.

Dr CS Li. Scientist, Chinese-Australian. Dr Li researched a method that controlled a form of rice parasite in 1965 – a contribution of world significance.

Alec Fong Lim was the first ethnic Chinese to be elected Lord Mayor of Darwin. This was in 1984.

Jenny Kee was a fashion designer and artist. She also painted. Her designs and art were often inspired by the Australian bush, and were full of those energetic colours. She was born at Bondi Beach in Sydney in 1947. Her father was Chinese, whose family came out to find gold in the 1850s. However, her mother was from the United Kingdom with Italian heritage. At school, she had to stand up for herself because she "looked" different to all the other kids, but Jenny felt it made her stronger. It also showed her that she was proud of who she was and of her mixed heritage.

Taking her creativity and love of fashion, she studied fashion design at Sydney. It was not long before her vibrancy in design had the "so called" experts telling her that her designs had too much colour for the staid Australian market… or that she should not wear her own designs – and just like those early racial comments, these remarks did not slow Jenny down. Wanting to expand her ideas, Jenny went to vibrant Britain, then the hub of pop music and fashion. London was good for Jenny as by being young, creative and talented she became well known. It was not long before she mixed in the "right" circles, meeting all sorts of "hi-flyers" She even met the Beatles. One report said, "London changed her life, the fashions were wild, and Jenny loved it." After seven whirlwind years, she wanted to return to Australia. Her confidence was high, she had a wonderful experience, and with that creativity, she wanted to make it in Sydney – and she did. It was not long before she opened her successful shop *Flamingo Park*. Her designs were quintessentially Australian, using colours out of the Australian bush. Focusing mainly on knitwear and textiles, it was not long before her pullovers were worn all over Australia. Marriage came (to artist Michael Ramsden), as did a daughter, Grace, and the family moved to the Blue Mountains, where she was even closer to the bush. She loved the trees, bush flowers (especially the Waratah) and the animals. Later, she became a passionate conservationist.

Jenny was a passenger on the well-known Granville Train when it crashed – she was changed for life. She and her daughter Grace survived when many did not. Whilst recovering, and as a way of coping, she started painting her much loved Australian flora and fauna. Many of these were painted on silk and were featured in *Italian Vogue*. Some were used by Chanel in Paris and Vogue Magazine called Jenny a National Fashion Icon – even Princess Diana wore her designs. Jenny's clothes, fabrics and designs are now part of the history of Australian fashion design. Jenny Kee passed away on 6th June 2012 aged 65. It is believed that she never fully recovered from the shock and stress of the train crash.

It is not known if Jenny visited China, but was known to follow Buddhism.

Claudia Cream was the first Chinese-Australian to be admitted (1980s) to the South Australia Supreme Court of the State in the early 1980s.

Russell (Goldfield) Jack founded the Golden Dragon Museum in Bendigo Victoria. The museum's website offers the following about it:

The Golden Dragon Museum, the 'Chinese Cultural Center of Australia'. The museum opened in 1991 to document, interpret and preserve the Chinese heritage in Australia…

A keen participant in life, Russell had numerous vocations such as a boiler maker and he also ran a Chinese restaurant.

In 1956, Melbourne Australia hosted the Olympic Games. Russell had the privilege of carrying the Olympic torch through his home town of Bendigo. Then forty-four years later he did the same for the 2000 Sydney Olympics. He was also the recipient of numerous awards for his work within the Bendigo Chinese Community as well as for the Golden Dragon Museum.

Among his awards were the Order of Australia medal and Meritorious Service in the Community, Victorian Awards for Excellence in Multicultural Affairs.

It was in Russell (Goldfield) Jack's Golden Dragon Museum where two famous innovators' works Loong and Sun Loong are displayed as mentioned above. (the Golden Dragon staff were most helpful in my research for this book)

Helen Sham in 1988 was the first Australian Chinese woman to win a seat in the Legislative Council of New South Wales.

Harry Chan rose to the position of President of the Legislative Council of the Northern Territory, the first Chinese person to hold this position and is not likely to be the last.

War

The Chinese Experience of War:

A speech by Senator Bill O'Chee Hansard (Senate of the Queensland {state} Parliament)

(refer above biography of Senator O'Chee's)

Senator O'CHEE's address, Thursday 10 November 1994:

> With Friday being Remembrance Day, and millions of Australians pausing at 11 am to remember the fallen of all wars, I feel it appropriate to draw to the attention of the parliament, and the Australian people, the contribution of our secret army in the First World War. The secret army to which I refer is that group of Anzacs (Australian and New Zealand Army Core 1914 – 1918) who were in fact ethnic Chinese and who, by virtue of the regulations of the day, were never meant to have been allowed to enlist in the first place.

It must be remembered that, prior to the outbreak of the war, Australia's first years of Federation were absorbed in part by the efforts of the unions and the Labor Party to impose the White Australia policy. This was because of the fear that Australia would be taken over by the Chinese... Against this background, therefore, the army at the outbreak of the First World War was obliged to reject, for anything other than non-combatant duties, any recruit who was not substantially of European origin or descent. The stupidity of these regulations can be seen in a letter written to the Argus by Mr. George Kong-Meng on 20 January 1916. To the Editor of the *Argus*.

> "Recruiting Stupidity"

> Sir, – Having answered the Prime Minister's appeal for recruits, I journeyed to Melbourne to offer my services to my country. I attended the recruiting depot at the Melbourne Town Hall on Friday, the 14th inst., and after giving my name, age and religion to the recruiting sergeant I was sent in with some others to the examining room, and told to undress, preparatory to the medical officer examining me as to my physical fitness. After my height, weight, and chest measurement had been taken by one of the officials there I was sent to the medical officer. Upon going before him I was told to get dressed again, and when I asked if I had failed to pass, the medical officer said he would not swear me in. When leaving the depot, I

received a certificate with 'not substantially of European origin' written on it, and signed by the medical officer, Captain N. J. Gerrard. With the exception of being asked where I came from, I was not asked one question whilst before the medical officer.

Now, sir, for your own guidance, I might state that my father was a British subject, born at Penang, S.S., and arrived in Australia in 1854. My mother was born in Tasmania in 1842, and I myself was born in this State in 1877. I have had six years' military training in the old Victorian Mounted Rifles, and 8th Australian Light Horse Regiment. My brother is at the front serving his King and country, having gone with the 1st Australian Division, and holds the rank of sergeant, but evidently the authorities at the Melbourne Town Hall depot seem to think I am not worthy of helping to defend the Empire. The Prime Minister has appealed to every man of military age to join the colours; but, if this is the treatment the native-born are to receive, I am afraid the appeal will fall on deaf ears. England and France deem it fit to use coloured troops to defend their shores, but the great Australian democracy denies its own subjects the same opportunities. I might state that I have gone to Melbourne on two occasions to offer my services to my King and country, and, after paying all travelling expenses, to be treated like this does not give one any encouragement to go again. – Yours, &c. George Kong-Meng Longwood, Jan. 20

The regulation was not only discriminatory but also ludicrous in light of the nationality of Australia's allies who were at that time fighting beside Australian troops in Gallipoli, in France and in the Palestine campaign, for they included Italians, Indians, Maoris and Japanese. In spite of these regulations, many ethnic-Chinese did enlist in the AIF and their heroism, bravery, and in some cases sacrifices, showed them to be truly the stuff of which the Anzac legend was made.

While it will never be known exactly how many ethnic Chinese enlisted, in part because Eurasians with European fathers are now impossible to identify, I wish to tell the tale of a number of these brave men to preserve forever the contribution they made to the forging of our nation.

One of those who enlisted at the outbreak of the war was William Edward 'Billy' Sing, who was born in Clermont in Queensland on 2 March 1886. His father John Sing was Chinese, born in Shanghai. His mother, Mary Ann Pugh, was born in England.

This small, dark man with the jet-black moustache may have been Eurasian but he was certainly not slow to enlist. His service number 355 shows that he was part of the original contingent of the 5th Light Horse. Arriving on the rocky shores of Gallipoli, he was assigned to the dreaded Quinn's Post, which was manned by

Up until the Second World War over 400 men of Chinese heritage fought for the Australian Armed Forces.

From the National Museum of Australia
Hundreds of Chinese Australians have served with Australian forces from the time of the Boer War (1899–1902), to the recent peacekeeping campaigns. During the Second World War (1939–1945) many Australians of Chinese origin enlisted in the Australian armed forces. It is estimated that there were probably more Chinese serving in the Australian forces than any other minority group in Australia. Women of Chinese descent also served. For instance, Phillis Anguey was a senior sister in the Royal Australian Air Force Nursing Service (RAAFNS) from 1940 to 1945, and Eunice Chin worked in the Australian Army Signal Corps.

From the Chinese-Australian's War Memorial in Dixon Street Sydney, one block away from the Sydney Chinatown

It was Thomas See who was the first Chinese-Australian to join the Royal Australian Air Force, moving up the ranks to serve as a bombing leader whilst flying long-range aircraft over the Atlantic.

Sydney's Chinatown Plaque

Queenslanders. Lest anyone think that all Chinese are short-sighted, with thick glasses, I should point out that Sing was a crack shot in an army of crack shots.

As a young boy growing up around Clermont, it is said that he was able to shoot the tails off piglets at 25 yards. So it is not surprising that he quickly gained a reputation as an extraordinary sniper who, during his time at Gallipoli, was officially credited with felling over 150 Turks and is believed to have accounted for a further 50 unofficial victims. It was Sing too, who won a deadly duel with the Turkish sniper known as Abdul the Terrible. In recognition of his achievements and bravery, he was awarded the Distinguished Conduct Medal and the Belgian Croix de Guerre.

Unfortunately, after returning to Australia, Billy Sing never did find a great fortune, although he did eke out a living on a gold lease before retiring to Brisbane where he died of a heart attack in 1943. Although he may not have been rich in monetary terms, there is no doubt that Billy Sing was rich in courage, spirit, and loyalty to his country. A few years ago, a plaque was placed on the wall of the warehouse, which now stands where Billy Sing passed away…

His incredible accuracy contributed greatly to the preservation of the lives of those with whom he served during a war always remembered for countless acts of valour and tragic carnage.

Not far away, another Chinese Australian, Lesley Henry Kew Ming was in action with the 23rd

Battalion and won the Military Medal at Polygon Wood. The citation reads, "Whilst digging the communication trench, he set a fine example to his men and encouraged them to satisfactorily complete the work though under heavy shellfire. He remained on duty though wounded until ordered to RAP."

Les Kew Ming is also interesting in that both his father Hi Kew Ming and his mother Louisa, the

daughter of local bootmaker Cum Moon, were Chinese Australians. In spite of this, he was given the opportunity to enlist and to serve his country, in no large doubt because of the attitude of a sympathetic local recruitment officer.

No doubt, a similar explanation is behind the enlistment of Walter Quan, who was born in Koondrook in Victoria to James and Ada Quan, and enlisted at Meekathara on 23 September 1915 where he stated his occupation to be a miner.

Quan's medical certificate upon enlistment stated him to be five foot nine and a quarter with a 37 inch chest, dark complexion, dark hair and blue eyes. I have seen a lot of Chinese and a lot of Eurasians, but I have never met one with blue eyes. Of course, if Quan's medical certificate said he had blue eyes, it was prima facie evidence that he was substantially of European descent. It was no doubt on that fiction that he was allowed to join up. Having completed his training, Quan was assigned to the 13th Reinforcement 16th Battalion on 17 December 1915 and embarked for Egypt on the Runic, arriving in Alexandria on 26 February 1916.

By this stage, the urgent need for men on the Western Front saw him transfer to the 48th Battalion and shipped to Marseilles on the Caledonia in June. In the murderous carnage around Pozieres, he was reported missing less than two months later on 8 August 1916 and now lies beside hundreds of his fellow Australians in Serre Road Cemetery in France. He was awarded the 1914–15 Star, the British War Medal and the Victory Medal.

When the war was over, surviving Chinese Australian Anzacs returned home to start a new life. Some, like Sam Tongway, found new opportunities open to them as a result of the training and education they received while in the forces.

In 1939, war broke out again. Chinese Australians again enlisted for the war in large numbers and served in all the forces. They were fighter pilots like Ray Goon, sailors like 'Bo' Liu, as well as soldiers. They even included amongst their number members of the elite Z Force such as Jack Sue. Some, like Wellington Lee, later went on to prominence in public life after leaving the services.

Others, while not enlisting in the army, navy or air force, enlisted in the merchant marine. According to Arthur Garlock Chang, who was the assistant secretary to the Chinese Seamen's Union and who came from the same village as my grandfather, as many as 2,000 Chinese served in the Australian merchant marine during the Second World War.

The speech I have been able to put together is not exhaustive, but it is a start.

I thank the Senate. The tales of the men I have mentioned are tales of courage, loyalty to Australia and honour to their families. The reason I have told their stories is not to raise them above other Anzacs Australian or New Zealanders in the army but to do them the service, which has been due to them for far too long – to honour their memory and their love of this country.

All Chinese Australians should be proud of the contribution their community has made to the building of our nation. On Remembrance Day, let us commemorate their sacrifice and be proud of the freedom they won for us.

Lest we forget.

Caleb James Shang is believed to have been the most highly decorated Chinese-Australian soldier. He served in the First World War and in the home defence in the Second World War. He was born in 1884, his mother

Jane Noon was from Gayndah, China, and his father, Lee Shang was from Guangdong, China. Caleb, being the eldest child left school at the age of twelve. Clearly, this did not hamper him.

Not often were people of Chinese heritage allowed to enlist in those days, but Caleb (and his brother) "snuck" in (he was awarded the Distinguished Conduct Medal (a decoration for gallantry in the field of war). He was also awarded the Military Medal (for bravery in battle). Until wounded, he was a sniper – and snipers, other than spies, were probably the most vulnerable of all soldiers. I remember reading a book on a famous South African sniper a few years ago, and what I learnt about snipers was incredible. Often times, they would hide buried in snow for a day before the enemy appeared. And they would have to lie there completely still, through all daylight hours with no food or toilet. Of course the enemy hated snipers and would do "whatever it took" to kill them.

Usually operating alone, using their marksmanship to "remove" specific targets, placed them in great danger. They operated under camouflage and stealth. But in modern times snipers are more about surveillance.

If that service was not dangerous enough, he also volunteered to be a signaller, which entailed sending messages using a signal lamp. He would sit on a hilltop, flashing messages with his lamp. At night the enemy would see the flashing light and would do their best to shoot the operator. Apparently, he was not a signaller, but found a signal lamp and could see the need to use it in the heat of battle and did so.

Another job was as a message runner, where he would run across horrendous battle fields with exploding shells, and bullets zinning all around, shattering lives. This entailed scouting close to, or even into, enemy positions to gain information.

Caleb must have stood out in the Australian army as few Asians were in the forces, but he would have been older than most because he enlisted at thirty-one years of age.

When he was awarded The Distinguished Conduct Medal (his first medal), Lieutenant Colonel A. P. Imlay, wrote:

This soldier displayed a contempt for danger and exhibited wonderful endurance and coolness resource and initiative and his conduct certainly inspired everybody he came in contact with ... His conduct throughout excited the admiration of officers and men.

From the Chinese-Australian's War Memorial Sydney (in other images below, you will notice the shape engraved on the corner plaque).

Sing was believed to have become the crack shot that he was as a result of hunting kangaroos as a youngster growing up in Australia.

Bo Liu enlisted with the Royal Australian Navy and was later appointed Captain's secretary.

Chinese-Australians also supported and made a valuable contribution to the war effort by building civil projects. One such job was where approximately 170 Chinese-Australians came from Sydney for the building of landing barges at the American military base in Brisbane.

Second Sino-Japanese War
In 1938 Australia supported China by blocking Japanese investment in Australia. The Japanese wanted to purchase an iron-ore mine in Australia as they wanted to secure the ore for armaments against China. Australia refused.

In 1943 Roy Goon became a squadron leader commanding the 83rd Squadron in the Royal Australian Air Force.

And his second citation General **John Gellibrand**, wrote:

> For conspicuous gallantry and devotion to duty ... and previous occasions. This soldier's example has always been a source of pride in this Battalion, but on this occasion, he excelled himself by his wonderful powers of endurance, intrepidity and utter contempt for danger. He volunteered for an O.P. in an advanced position at the start of operations and maintained it throughout until attack started when he reaped a harvest with his rifles until his post was blown right out. He came back through enemy fire to get more rifles but was employed as a runner and made several trips through enemy barrage, which was intense. He continued carrying ammunition and running until company moved out when he volunteered to remain behind and cover retirement with a Lewis Gun, which he did successfully. He showed an utter disregard for danger and is a gallant soldier.

And later, for his **Military Medal**, Colonel **Raymond Leane**, stated:

At VILLERS BRETONNEUX on 1st May, 1918, he displayed remarkable bravery and initiative in making a daylight reconnaissance of the Sector under heavy Machine Gun fire and snipers' activities and which proved of considerable value to us. He established an O.P. at which he was continually sniped at and succeeded in conveying back valuable information of enemy movement and directed our artillery fire on to the enemy formations causing them many casualties. He maintained this Post during tour in line without relief.

After he recovered from his wounds (this took many months), and upon arriving home, Shang received a hero's welcome, with large crowds and many dignitaries to welcome him.

According to his sister (Fang Yuen), Shang would not talk about the war, and certainly not about his gallantry.

Sadly he never really recovered and was in and out of hospital for years.

Caleb James Shang First World War – Western Front

- Battle of Bullecourt
- Battle of Messines
- Battle of Menin Road
- Battle of Polygon Wood
- Battle of Passchendaele
- Defence of Amiens
- Battle of Amiens

Photo of Caleb James Shang with the kind permission of Cairns Historical Society

A list of around 400 names have been researched and listed

The main commendation

The main commendation from a different angle.

Chinese-Australian War Memorial
This permanent memorial, recognising the contribution to all the Australian war efforts by Chinese-Australians is on the corner of Dixon and Liverpool streets, at the entrance of Sydney's China town.

Cai's Epic – A story

The below story is my story of the gold rush days. I offer the story to give you a better feel and perspective of what the early Chinese-Australians went through. It commences in the 1850s in China.

Wang Cai straightened his back to ease the tension. He had been bending over for hours. Although only twelve years old, most of his young life he had been working the fields with his father (Fuqin and now his younger brothers. Some of the village children went to the Confucius School but his family were more concerned with feeding themselves, therefore he worked. At this time of the year, the ground was hard to work because it was often frozen – yet they toiled. If they could not produce enough yams, they'd go hungry. The farming methods they used had been used for generations.

Hearing a commotion, he saw his second sister running towards them, calling him and Father. Worried, Father ran towards her. 'What is the matter Second Daughter?' She told him that there were two merchants at their house.

'They want to see you Father and the first boy.'

Father knew it would be a waste of time asking her what it was about but instead called for Cai.

'Come, hurry, there is important business.'

Upon arriving, he saw the two visitors in the kitchen in the warmest seats, the place of honour. They had been given tea by his wife and what morsels of food that could be spared. He knew they could not afford to give this away but respect dictated that they did. They would have to borrow and pay back from where they could.

After the formalities, the men got down to business. Father did not say much but listened and often nodded his head. Cai did not understand what it was all about. Every so often, he heard the word Aodaliya (the traditional Chinese word for Australia. However, Australia, as explained earlier in this book had not come into being as a country at that stage). Therefore, they were really talking about the colony of Victoria and Dai Gum San.

'Cai, go back to the field, I need to talk to Mother (Muqin).' He did as he was told and as he walked back, he had a feeling of unease. He knew his life was about to change, but had no comprehension of what that change could mean.

That night his parents were quiet, keeping their thoughts to themselves as they had their meal. Cai was too respectful to ask questions. After dinner, Father told the children to go to their beds except for Cai. Father said nothing for fully fifteen minutes. Cai waited, trying to be patient. Suddenly Father broke the silence.

'Number One Son... you have a duty to do for your parents, your grandparents, and your brothers and sisters. You will go to a place called Aodaliya. I don't know of this place... but you go to the Dai Gum San. You must make money and send it back home... You are not the first of our people to do this... You must do this.'

Cai said, 'I am honoured to do this Father', but his mind screamed. *NOOOOOOOOOOOOO. I can't leave you my Father or Mother, my grandparents, or my brothers and sisters. This is my home, this is all I know, I belong here... with you all.* He knew, that as the Number One Son that it was his duty, to his venerable parents and grandparents. He must accept this with honour and respect. 'When do I go Father?'

'In four days' time.'

'But we have no money Father, how do we pay for the transport to this place called Aod..od....'

'Aodaliya,' pronounced his father. 'Those two merchants will organise it and pay your way. They will help you find work. And then you will pay them back.'

Cai was silent, his mind working every which way, like locusts consuming a field. Then in a rush he asked, 'Where is this place, is it far? How do I get there?'

'It is far, very far, so far, I do not understand... You go by carriage to a boat. Then on the boat... I don't know how long. Then you walk for a short distance, a day or two.'

'And the people. Are they nice, like in our village?'

'I... I don't know... They may not be like us... They don't look like us, they are pale, like rotten milk, with long noses that make them look strange. Their eyes do not have our beautiful shape... They may be... barbarians... (yeman ren).'

'Barbarians… No Father. I can't…'

'Be quiet… you will do your duty. Your mother and I have decided. You go… and do us honour.'

It was at this stage that his mother came out, but she could not look at her Number One Son. She busied herself with cleaning. At one stage, Father went outside to relieve himself and Cai cried out 'Mother…' but he got no further as she waved him to be quiet whilst blurting out, 'Father has spoken. You will honour the family.' Her voice wavered, and he noticed a tear in her eye.

'Go to bed, you must be in the field early tomorrow.'

Sitting there, with the flickering candles, he felt tears coming to his eyes and ten-thousand butterflies in his stomach. He had to go outside, he could not show her his fear, as it would displease his mother. Hurrying outside, he bumped into his father who was returning, but he did not stop and ran out into the grounds and to the lake. Although cold, he did not feel it…. *I will never sleep in the same bed as my brothers, never play in the trees with them… why me, why?*

Inside Mother looked at Father but he cut her off, 'Don't cry for Number One Son, that one is strong, he is just young. He has more power in his mind than a hundred Number One Sons. He will do better than most.'

'But… he is so young,' the mother said.

***

It was soon enough that the driver shouted for the horses to go. Cai turned around to see his family, and village one last time. *Will I ever see this again he wondered, my parents, grandparents, and siblings… and my uncles and aunties… all twenty-five of them*? He watched them all becoming smaller and smaller as the carriage drew further away, until he saw them no more.

***

Lost in remorse he did not remember much of this part of the trip, other than the fact that most of the passengers were about his age – *these children should be heading to school, not a land so far away*.

They travelled for nine days until they reached the harbour that they were to sail from. The ship, *Kuaisu de yueliang* was a two-master. 'That?' He said to the boy next to him. 'We are going on the sea in that, far away, on that tiny thing?' Against the wharf, he paced it out. Only thirty-eight of his largest paces. 'I hope we don't have big waves.'

They joined a queue of about sixty others. Some were men going to seek the gold mountain. There, at what he was later to learn was a gangplank was one of the two merchants that recruited him. He remembered at his house that the merchants were friendly and jovial. They smiled a lot to encourage. Now, this one was different, he was scowling and shouted orders as he checked the name of each person against a list. When Cai reached him and gave his name, 'Wang Cai', he then asked politely, 'How long is our voyage to take Sir?'

The merchant growled, 'It'll take as long as it takes… move on… next.'

Up the gangplank Cai went, with his few possessions in a bag slung over his shoulder. Gone was the food his mother gave him to see him on his way. On deck, the ship looked even smaller. 'Down you go, through that door and down those steps. At the bottom find a place that you call yours.' As he started to descend, he realised that the voice was the other merchant.

With each downward step it got darker, air heavy with rot assaulted his lungs. It felt like a rat hole. Later that proved to be the case. It took a few minutes for his eyes to get use to the gloom so he could find a space but he still tripped over a few men on the way.

Being all from the same region, they could understand each other and so conversations sprung up.

Cai kept close to Fuju who was from his village. They had grown up together and so made sure they were next to each other. As they talked quietly between themselves, they swore an allegiance to support each other. Fuju took out a knife and gave them both a small cut where they joined their blood.

Soon others joined in the conversation. One of the men said he had overheard that they were to sail at high tide the next day. Another moaned that he was hungry and wondered when he was to get fed. From the other side of the hull, which was only about twenty feet, a voice said that he needed to relieve himself and wondered where to do this.

'In that bucket,' a different voice said. 'That's where you go. Not very big for all of us.'

An hour later men still kept coming down those stairs, and with each one, the men had to crowd closer together until there was no room for a grain of rice between them. The air became thinner and more putrid.

The door suddenly slammed shut and they heard a timber brace placed. This caused shouting and panic. All the banging and shouting made no difference. The door remained secured. Many of the men, or rather the children, had spent their entire life in the fields in the open fresh air, and to be entombed was too much to bear. Cai told Fuju not to panic or shout to preserve their strength, saying the air would get thinner.

For some two hours they sat in the blackness until they heard the timber being lifted and the door open. The first man they saw had a stick, which he used on those who tried to get out. He only had to whack a few heads for the message to get through. Three or four men entered, each carrying two buckets. A man they had not seen before accompanied them. He was Chinese and had the accent of the south. He shouted for quiet. When all were quiet, he called himself Zhang Chong.

He said, 'I am like one of you, but the bosses used me to interpret their words.' Continuing, he said, 'They lock the doors to stop anyone from leaving the ship, but when underway the doors will be left opened.' He explained that the within the buckets was their food and that they must enjoy it as they will not get any more until they sailed.

Another man came with metal cups for the food. As fast as they came in, they were back out the door and the door made secure once more.

The first man to taste the food spat it out... 'Shit... this is shit.'

Another announced, 'We give our pigs better than this.'

Fuju said that he would rather not eat but Cai said, 'You must. The food may make you feel sick, but not eating it will make you feel sicker.' Through that evening Cai came to the realisation *that it was now up to him, that he could only survive through his efforts. He could not rely on another.*

Being so dark, the only way they could keep track of the time was because one man could see through a slither of a crack between the door. He announced that it was night. Even so, there was not much sleeping. There was not enough room and too much fear. The talking did not stop, most were panicked. A few of the younger ones, such as Gongshi, could be heard crying. At first, he tried to control himself, but as time went by he openly wept, calling for his father and his mother. He was fearful and could not be consoled.

Suddenly there was a curse, 'La shi', it seemed that one man was bitten by a rat that had run over him. Realising that the rat was on him, he tried to brush it away with his hands but the razor sharp teeth snapped. The man kept complaining that the bleeding would not stop.

After what seemed like several days, it was announced that the night had elapsed, as it was now daylight. 'Good', said a voice, 'we should be going soon, and the doors will open.' No such thing, as they could feel the boat rolling and banging against the wharf. Wind was heard whistling through the timbers. Because of the storm, the ship remained in port. Nor did the doors open, no food was delivered, and no one came to collect the latrine buckets.

Time was announced by the man at the crack… three times he announced, 'Day', and three times 'Night'. The men were hungry, many were sick and weak. The man who had been bitten was delirious. With each day, the men got weaker and sicker. At last, they felt the ship settle, and the wind abate. As light came there were many feet on the deck above them that suggested activity. Muffled shouts and orders could be heard, whilst feet ran back and forth. As the daylight became stronger they felt the ship take on a different movement. No longer was there a rhythm of the ship rising and descending against the wharf, now there was a sideways roll as it started to surge.

As the surge got faster, one man shouted in panic, 'It's leaking, water's coming in!' Some tried to block it, but it was like trying to hold up the rain.

Still the door did not open. Adding to the misery, seasickness caused many to vomit. Whether it was the food, or the conditions, some got diarrhea. Cai suggested to Fuju to put a cloth over his nose to stop the smell. Then later, 'Listen everyone', Cai shouted, 'listen to me. All of you with staffs or cups or even your feet, start banging on the deck above. We have to remind them we are here and we will not stop until they open the door and bring food and water.'

The noise inside the hull was deafening but on deck, it was muffled, but still loud enough for each of the crew to hear it. The noise in the captain's cabin was almost as loud as where the men were. Still the door did not open. Again, Cai shouted, 'We will take shifts. Now every second person must bang for ten minutes. Then we will swap.'

After two hours, the captain ordered the doors to be opened. He had never encountered this behaviour on previous trips. Half an hour later, food and water were carried down. The doors remained opened but two guards with sticks were placed at the opening to ensure no one left.

When the latrine buckets had not been replaced, once again it was Cai who spoke, 'They don't empty the buckets, then we will. Come Fuju, ... and who else? They carried the buckets up the steps, and just before the opening, they hurled the contents out the door and onto the deck. The two guards swore, as some of the muck splashed onto them. The empty buckets were replaced ready for use. Thereafter, three times a day crew came and collected the full buckets.

They counted the days as they passed. Twice the ship pulled into a port, but they were never allowed up on deck. At least with the door open and the latrine buckets emptied on a regular basis, things were tolerable for those who were not sick. After the twelfth day, the man who had been bitten died. His body was removed, presumably, thrown over the side. Two days later another died. This was a young boy who was one of the first to cry when the doors were first locked. Many were sick.

For his lot Cai felt weak, but he knew he would recover. *They lied to Father. If he knew of this he would not have let them take me.*

NB, by studying the map on the front cover you will see the direction that most of the boats took.

***

Finally, after thirty-five days at sea, and three days in port, they felt the ship being docked. By that time, five more had died.

It was not long after that they were called on deck and were directed down the gangplank where they were soon to be addressed by one of the merchants. It felt strange being on a stable wharf without the rocking motion. They were a sorry looking lot that supported each other. Many were holding their hands to their eyes to stop the assault of the bright glare of the Australian sun after thirty-five days of darkness.

The merchant announced, 'You are in Port Adelaide.'

Many shouted, 'We are supposed to be in Melbourne... some thousand kilometres further along.'

'We drop you here because the government of Victoria demands that you pay a tax of ten pounds to enter Victoria. Ten pounds is more than one year's earnings. By dropping you off here, we save you that money. You do have a few days walk to get to the Dai Gum San in Bendigo.

To help you along the way I have paid a guide. He will go with you and show you the way… and Chang will also go with you as he speaks English and will translate for you. You will be leaving in half an hour. There is food for you to eat now, and some for you to take. I will meet you at Dai Gum San in Bendigo, where I will help you find work. Remember, you must do this because you have a debt to pay, to honour your parents. If you do not pay you bring disrespect to your family… and your family will become responsible for your debt if you do not honour it.'

There was a shocked murmur from the men. One man asked, 'How much do we have to pay you?'

The answer was, '50% of your first two years of service, payable each time you get paid.'

'Two years?' They shouted. 'That is too much.'

The merchant replied, 'Why, how much do you think it cost to get you here, the carriage, the ship, and food. We have given you an opportunity to honour your family. You will all get rich…' He was not able finish.

'That was not food, it was pig's slop.'

Another shouted, 'You rob us, it is too harsh.'

Cai saw no point in arguing with the greedy merchants and said nothing.

As they ate, many were disgruntled. They were all given some flour to last them for the trip, and told to use it sparingly. There was water on the horses, but they got one cup in the morning and two cups at night, where one of those cups was to make the flour damper.

'What is damper?' many asked, but they were told they would learn soon enough.

They were instructed that every day they would leave at dawn and walk until about noon. There they would rest during the worst of the heat of the day, until three pm, and then they would walk until it was too dark to see.

They learnt that they had travelled so far from home that their seasons were opposite to those at home. Where it is winter there, it was the height of summer here. They had no way of knowing or taking the temperature, but in Celsius it was already thirty degrees, and it was only nine am. The guide who sat atop a horse shouted, 'This way, follow me'. This was translated by the interpreter Chong.

From their starting point, it was flat and swampy, and so the going was slow. Little did they know their three day walk would take much longer than that, and some would not make it. After two hours they stopped to rest under some trees… gum trees the guide called them. They would learn that Australia is full of these. They were beyond the swampy area of the coastal region, and the land was dry and arid. It undulated, but with a slight rise as they moved further inland. Except for the heat it was easy walking. Cai kept considering what it would be like to grow food on the land.

Now the sun was high, and each breath was like sucking from a furnace, throats were parched. On that first break they were stunned and frightened as an Aboriginal tribesman suddenly appeared. No one saw him approach, he was just there, black as mahogany. His face carried the harshness of the climate, looking like the bark of some of those gum trees. He had no clothes but a kind of belt or carry-sack around his waist. He was tall and sinewy, like the ligaments of the duck they ate at home. He seemed to float across the ground. With a beard, and markings on his chest, he looked ancient, and fierce. He carried a spear in one hand and a club in the other.

With him, Cai was fascinated to see a dingo (wild dog) at his feet. With all these people, the dingo was wary, with ears permanently erect, giving it an intelligent look. It was ginger-coloured with a white chest. Cai noticed that the teeth were much larger than normal dogs. Later he learnt that the dingo is the largest meat-eating mammal in Australia. They followed the early human migration from Asia across the land bridge many thousands of years earlier.

In his language, he tried to speak to the Guide but the gestures of the Guide were hostile, and the men could see that the guide told the bushman to get away.

He did not, he went and sat under a gum tree about a hundred metres away and kept watch. When they resumed their journey, the Aboriginal followed but kept his distance. Every so often though, he would wander off or disappear, his dingo with him.

Just before dark, the Guide, through Chong the interpreter, called all the men to collect wood for their fires as they walked. Half an hour later, they stopped for the day. They were shown how to make a fire.

Did you know that it is 9,113 kilometres between Melbourne and Beijing? It is a further 600 kilometres to Hobart. The closest points between the two countries are Darwin to Taiwan, which is 4,160 kilometres. Cai and the men would have travelled between 6,000 and 7,000 kilometres in that leaky boat.

China has a land mass of roughly 21% larger than Australia.

One report said, It's estimated 17,000 Chinese, mostly men, traversed from South Australia by foot to Victoria.

But not all went by foot as this image shows. These would have been the few with funds as most could not afford the high costs (image supplied by **www.slv.vic.gov.au**). The carrier was Australia's well-known and well-loved Cobb & Co.

Gum trees There are over 700 species of gum trees. They are also a very useful tree. Where I only give a few uses that the indigenous people made use of the tree (later in the story), but currently it is also used for: allopathic medicine, insecticides, insect repellent, fragrances, anti-fungicides and more recently for fuel. Most of this is from the extracted oil.

Gum tree in flower curtesy of Pixabay and https://en.wikipedia.org/commons

The Guide called the men to come to him and watch.

'Damper,' he said, 'is a famous Australian recipe that the bush travellers have used ever since they came.'

As the Guide took out the flour and got water, Chong explained.

'This place is called Australia, not Aodalia, as you call it.'

Continuing the demonstration, the Guide said, 'You put in a mixing tin one cup of flour, and a pinch of salt. Add half a cup of water. This is not enough for one person, so for each person to mix double. Each man must be in a group of about eight people, as you will take turns to cook – besides, we only want one fire a night. Fire is bad in Australia, especially at this hot time of year, and so you must be very careful.' He said this twice. 'Did you get this?' he asked.

'Shi shi,' they said and nodded their heads.

'Next, you mix it, and take it out of the tin, and put on a piece of gum bark and roll it, just like your mother used to make…?'

'Mainbao,' Chong offered.

More 'Shi shis.'

'Now feel this texture,' he passed it around for many to feel. They knew this texture. Then using a stick, he separated some coals from the fire and placed the damper on these before scraping more coals over the top, covering the damper. 'It takes about thirty minutes. When ready, you pull it apart, give each man an even portion. You will eat half tonight, and the rest tomorrow… it is nutritious and fills the gut.' He said this whilst he patted his stomach.

When they had all tasted their efforts, many thought the smoky, crusty flavour enjoyable. As the trip continued, the more enterprising of them used different grasses or roots from which to add flavours.

***

Death by a dingo?
A famous episode in Australian history was of the baby girl Azaria Chamberlain in 1980.

The family had been camping near Uluru (Ayres Rock) when, apparently a dingo went into the tent and took off with the baby. The body was never recovered. For many years the legal system, and the Australian public thought the mother had killed the child. She was convicted of murder and was to spend life in prison. However, after three years in prison, fragments of the child's clothes were (fortuitously) found in a dingo lair some distance from where she was taken, and so the mother was released.

A well attended movie was made of the event, as were many documentaries, with several books on the matter.

It is now believed by most that little Azaria's death was due to a dingo.

Dingo (supplied by Pixabay)

Dingo (supplied by Pixabay)

Fully dark now, they saw a fire in the distance. 'The Aboriginals,' some murmured. Most kept a wary eye on the fire to see if the ancient one came nearer. They were concerned and thought that he bought bad spirits with him. It had been bad enough already, with seven dying, and the hardships… and that wild dog of his, straight from the bad spirits. They did not want more trouble and so took turns to keep watch on him and his wild companion.

Cai did not think this First Australian was of bad Shui, and so after finishing his half of the damper, and carefully wrapping up the rest in a cloth, he said that he was going to look at the stars. He had never seen so many. He looked for the familiar constellations of his home, none could be seen, replaced with these unrecognisable one. *What a strange place this Australia is* he thought before wandering to the campfire of the black one.

Before getting there, the dingo gave an aggressive growl. Cai later learnt that dingoes do not bark, their throat was not developed to bark. The black one chuckled, a friendly gesture. He indicated that Cai sit down next to his fire. The black one spoke in his language, which of course Cai could not understand, but he did understand the friendly gesture. To be polite he thanked the man. Both laughed, knowing that one could not understand the other. The dingo still kept a low growl, but a stern poke with a stick by its owner soon settled it. For a time they were quiet, but then the black man offered Cai a piece of meat that he had cooked. It was a fish of some type, then Cai remembered the man wandering off on occasions… *of course this man would know the land and how to live off it*. The fish was dry and tasted good. He indicated that it was good and a gesture of bowing his head in thankfulness. After more silence, the man suddenly grabbed Cai's arm, not in a manner of aggression, but with concern and spoke in agitation. By the light of the fire, Cai watched the gestures of the man – he indicated the Guide on his horse, that something bad was to befall him. Cai did not know what to think of this and said, 'Huai' several times (bad, bad).

More silence, then several times, pointing to his own chest, Cai said, 'Cai, me Cai… Cai,' then indicated for his friend to say his name.

The man understood and said, 'Anatjarri,' poking his chest several times. 'Anatjarri… Antjarri.'

Cai said, 'You Atjarr, me Cai.'

Shaking his head, the black man slowly said, 'Anat…jarri… Anatjarri.' Once again, Cai mispronounced it, but after a time he was able to call him Jarri. The big black face laughed, white teeth in the dark. He also pronounced Cai with an accent on the C, but both settled on the pronunciations, and once again they chuckled.

The **Dingo Fence** was erected thirty years after Cai and his men arrived in Australia. It was built to control the roaming packs of the hunting dingoes to protect the flocks of sheep.

It is the longest fence in the world (5,614 kilometers), and is even almost double the length of the Great Wall of China.

Thousands of dingoes perished through starvation because of the wall and their interrupted hunting paths.

The Dingo fence – image complements; Peter Woodard

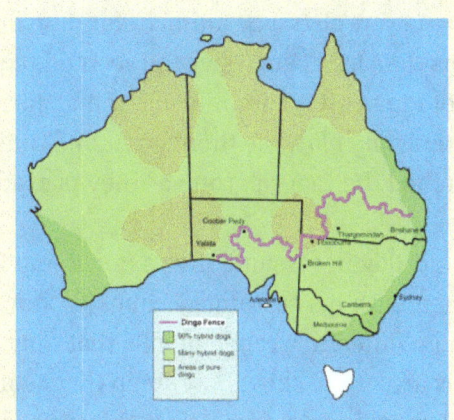

The Dingo fence map – image Wikimedia Commons

After a time Cai stood up and kau-taued to the man and waved thanks before heading back to his camp and hopefully sleep. The dingo followed him half way before standing and watching Cai away from his territory.

***

They headed off at the first sign of daylight, a motley bunch. Half starved, many still sick. There was no choice but to put one foot in front of another for another two days. What would happen after the two days… what then, they wondered?

Cai looked for Jarri and there he was. The dog forever at his side. Both men put up their hands in a distant greeting, a recognition of the other. The day was going to be hotter than yesterday, probably because they were moving away from the coastal breeze. The Guide kept shouting at them to hurry up – 'at this rate we'll all be old men before we get there'. They could only go as fast as the weakest. Many were struggling, but not Cai, he was too intrigued by the surroundings to feel poorly. He saw all sorts of birds that he had never seen before, many with an array of bright colours, where the songs, or screeching held his attention for hours. Every so often, he saw a strange animal, standing upright, on two back legs, with smaller front legs that were more like arms than legs. A massive tail seemed to propel the hoping motion. He watch one as it scratched its belly, like an old man after climbing out of bed. Jarri said it was called a kan-ger-roo. *A most interesting creature. A most interesting place,* he thought. At one time, they walked past more Indigenous people, but they just stood and watched the ragged group as they passed. They made no greetings or smiles… just watched.

At the mid-day break, and after a quick nap Cai went and saw Jarri. Jarri indicated that it was easy walking now. Then with his customary chuckle, showed that it was soon going to be uphill. Then, as if to prove the point, he pointed to a range of hills that only just showed above the horizon. Cai had not noticed these. Jarri move his arm up to show how steep they would be. 'Biaoda guanqie,' was all Cai could say. Jarri showed that it would be two more days before they would get there.

'Two days? They said it would only take three days and we have been walking for a day and a half already.' Of course, Jarri did not understand this. Once again, Jarri warned Cai of the impending doom of the guide. Not quite believing this, and not wanting to worry the men, he said nothing about it.

When he went back to the main camp, he went to the interpreter Chong and demanded he take him to talk to the Guide to speak. 'We were told that it would only take three days, but it seems like it will be much longer.'

Wombats are shy marsupials native to Australia. Up to a meter long, with short legs and a muscular body, they look like furry tanks. They are the closest relative to the koala bear.

The First Australians used the meat and the fur. A strange phenomenon of the wombat is its cubed shape droppings. The droppings are used to mark their territory, and being cube-shaped helps to keep the dropping where they are dropped, and not roll off a rock.

Moreover, a group of wombats is called a wisdom of wombats.

Wombats. This one scurrying across the road, which is how we see most of them. (Above)Mother and baby sharing dinner (Photos curtsey of; https://en.wikipedia.org/wiki/Wombat)

'Who told you that?' asked the Guide... 'Never mind, it will take ten to fifteen days.'

It only took ten minutes for the news to circulate through the Chinese encampment. When it was time to start walking, it did not matter how many times the Guide called them, they remained sitting. There was muttering amongst them. One of the oldest amongst them said, 'We can't walk for ten more days'.'

When the Guide came over with the interpreter and asked, 'What's the problem', no one spoke, but they all looked to Cai, even the older men, and gestured. 'You tell him.'

Cai was not sure that he was wise or confident enough to be the selected spokesperson for the group, and once standing he looked at the ground and shuffled his feet in uncertainty.

'Sir,' he directed his gaze to the guide, whilst the interpreter gave the words to the guide. 'We are simple people and come from small villages in China... This land,' at this he gave a gesture with his arms to indicate the vast horizon around them. 'We... we don't understand it... and on the ship... Sir, things were not good, we were told only a few days, but we were on it for many days, no proper food, men sick... seven die. Now, we are weak and tired but we have to... walk for ... too far... yes, too far. We have been given little to eat, not enough... and too little water, two cups a day... yet, it is hot. If we go on like this more of us will die.' At this, many murmured acknowledgement. The Guide nodded his head in understanding. 'If we die, or are weak, then your bosses will not collect their bounty on us... this suites none. For us to go on, we need more water, more food. We need rest.'

Once again, he was interrupted by the approval of what was being said. For the first time since the merchants came to their village did they feel that they had a voice, and that they were being heard.

Now, Cai was getting to his proposition... they would not move until more food and water was to be given to them. He did not want to seem to be aggressive, and rather to appeal to the guide for assistance. So he said nothing more and waited for the guide to speak. He would know within the first few words if this man was fair or not, whether he wanted to help or was he just a tool of the bosses who paid his wage.

Uncertain, the Guide was not keen to speak, but knowing there was no avoiding it, he cleared his throat. 'Chinamen. I see that you are sick, and slow to walk... I... I had nothing to do with how much food you have been given... same with water. It is true that there are many days of walking. So all that you say is correct. ...But it is difficult... my job is to take you to Bendigo... the place of much gold... and that is what I will do. I can't produce more flour... or water for you, but I can show you the way... and that is what I am going to do.'

The **Brushtail possum** is a nocturnal marsupial that is native to Australia. Their diet mostly consists of the leaves of the gumtrees, but they sometimes eat the meat of small animals.

Not only seen in the bush, they live in cities and towns, city parks and residential areas, where often they are regarded as pests as they do damage to gardens, fruit trees and under-house wiring and plumbing. But as a protected species it is illegal for householders to hurt or kill them.

A fully-grown possum, and a youngster. Being nocturnal, they are out for a meal. Photo curtesy of Wikipedia Commons

I found this baby when on a hike in South Australia. He was close to death, very cold and hungry. Probably only a week old, and most likely fell out of the tree above. I took him to an animal shelter. When I phoned back two weeks later I was told that he was fine. They also said that if I found him two hours later he would have been dead.

The aim was to release him back into the wild, but they could not do this on his own, as he would not survive. They had other young possums, and so they put them together to form their own wisdom (collective unit), and when ready, all would be released into an area where there were no competing wisdoms.

One man of about fourteen, and even though only fourteen, was surely now a man, as all traversed from boyhood to manhood in these few short weeks, shouted, 'Then you walk, and we all ride your horse.' There was much laughing at this.

The guide merely said, 'I ride now… if you want to live, you follow me… now!' With that, he climbed on his horse. Quickly Cai assessed his options, the eyes of the men on him. He saw Jarri on the edge of the camp, he in turn seemed to know what was happening and he raised his spear in a gesture of strength. 'Sir, then you go on your own. We Chinamen, as you call us, would rather die with our self-respect here, than follow you to a death of agony. So you go and leave us.'

He turned to the interpreter and nodded, 'You too, we don't want boss's men here.' It was then that some of the men stood up, and pointed for the Guide and the interpreter to get going. 'Leave us.'

Cai then went to the interpreter and said, 'Go now, I want to talk to them men without your big ears listening.' A few of the men forcibly took Chong's arms and determinedly walked him about thirty metres away, and said, 'Go… go further. You are not even from our part of the country… you are not one with us.'

'Sit down men and listen to me,' Cai said. What I said to that longnose is not what it really is. Yes, he can go and you may think that we will perish here… but that will not happen as we still have enough food and water to go back the way we came from, back to Port Adelaide… in two or three days we will be back at the place where the ship came. There must be food there. And if the merchants are still there we can demand food, after all, there are fifty-three of us, and they can't ignore us.' Seeing the logic of this clever young man, all cheered, they knew he was right.

Whilst this was taking place, the Guide was uncertain and had not moved. He was not a bad man, and did not want anyone in his care to perish. He had his duty, and it was this ping-pong game of indecision that pre occupied him. To follow orders or be more humane. His decision made, he quickly rode to the interpreter, and said, 'Come, there is more talking.'

As he got back to the crowd, he climbed off his horse, so as not to seem to be looking over them. Then said, 'This is what I will do. You wait here for me, and I will ride back to Port Adelaide. I will somehow convince the bosses to give more food and water. You have my word'. Everyone cheered, many slapped Cai on the back in acknowledgement of this win. From that time onwards, Cai had been accepted as the champion of the people of his country. But Cai was smart enough to know that this was only one win. There would be many fights in the future, of that he was sure.

Kangaroos

When anyone thinks of Australia, they think of kangaroos. Did you know that they come in lots of different sizes such as those in the photos? There are also tree kangaroos, which are about the size of a small child's thumb.

The larger roos, as they are referred to, are the largest hopping animal in the world; so proficient, they can hop up to 70km per hour, covering ten meters in a jump or go over a four-metre fence. They are also good swimmers. I once saw some swimming, to and from, an island that was several hundred metres off shore as there was good grazing there. They are smart as well, as often they went at low tide as there was less swimming and more hopping.

Kangaroos were important to the indigenous people as they used the meat, the fur for clothing, bedding and mats, the sinews for sowing and tying and the bones for tools/clubs.

Sadly, roughly 2.1 million roos are mowed down on the road each year. Seldom do they survive a car hit, especially at speed. Worse, is when the mother is carrying a joey (baby roo) in its pouch. I remember speaking to a panel beater (from a rural area) and he said that two thirds of the cars he repairs are damaged by roos! Wildlife reports reveal that there are approximately 2.4 million animal deaths a year on the road. Then insurance figures give that 88% of these are kangaroos.

Whilst the kangaroo may be an iconic animal for Australia, many Australians feel the same about the pandas of China – we love them and want to know more about them.

This one is a Wallaby, a species of kangaroo (Wikipedia Commons).

Kangaroo and joey (baby) (Wikipedia Commons).

Once again, the Guide climbed his horse, 'I will go now, and should be back there by dark tonight. It may take me two days to get the supplies, and another full day to return... expect me in four days. Meanwhile, I leave the water and all the flour. Know, in this land, water is more precious than the gold you seek, so appoint someone to issue it out with caution. In the meantime, you rest under these trees and heal your sickness.' With that he took off at a good pace.

Cai trusted the Guide to fulfil his promise. From this, he learnt that there are good men, and bad men, and he must learn quickly how to judge both. Once again, he looked at Jarri, who raised his spear to show he knew he had done well. This prompted Cai to wonder *and of course, there is this land, and the Aboriginals... who are they? He knew he would find out.*

***

Over the four days, most of the men recovered their strength, but three did not and passed to their ancestors. It was a sad time for all. Within the group they collected joss sticks, and some had statues of their deities. Some collected the wild flowers that grew around, and so a shrine was created from which to give the dead men a proper send off. Cai looked for the most reverent of the men and asked if he would be their spiritual leader. His name was Fong. Within their ceremony, they included the man, who had died from the rat bite, and the young boy who also died, as well as the other five. It was a solemn time, but one of affirming who they were as people. They may have been in a strange land, but they still had the knowledge of who they were.

They now also had a priest and he was to set up the shrine at the end of every day's march. Later, in that place called Bendigo, it was Fong who created the first temple there for the people to gain spiritual sustenance and guidance – and when they had their first Chinese New Year celebrations, it was Fong who did the blessings.

On the third day of resting, Cai asked Fuji to count and check the number of men. One was missing, it was Gongshi. He was a boy who came from the village next to Cai's. One minute he was there, the next he was gone. Worried, Cai went to Jarri, who stayed by the camp site. The dingo was never far from him. Explaining as best as he could, he asked Jarri if he could find the missing man. Without saying a word, Jarri walked around the men, as if a big circle, all the while scanning the ground, often on haunches, sometimes sniffing, and sometimes feeling (Cai was to learn later, that this feeling that they had was called "Miwe" and was a most profound skill). Suddenly, Jarri stood tall, before pointing in a direction. He then headed that way, the dog trotting after him.

The following is what Cai found out about this land; *It was a place of desert and gums. The place teemed with animals - kangaroos and wallabies jumped with ease and power. Possums, the bushy-tailed cats of the gum tree gallivanted at night, where they preened and squabbled with a low-sounding growl. Light-pawed, they gracefully leapt from branch to branch, tree to tree. In the day they slumbered in tree stumps.*

There is an abundance of bird varieties, amongst the largest and the most colourful in the world, parakeets, galas, cockatoos and hundreds of others. At a later time, Cai would think one can never be lonely in this bush because of the constant racket of warbles, tweets and all other manner of bird conversation, he grew to love them. He was not sure of his favourite, the magpie with its lyrical and changing parley or the Kookaburra with its laugh of "aaaaaAhooaaaaaKKkoooAAhooo" that could be heard a kilometre away. At first, its raucous shrills sent a chill up his and the men's spine... Jarri laughed at this.

It is an old land and so are its people. Some say it has 68,000 years of continuous habitation – a hardy race that knows the land, a race that has formed strong spiritual connections from observation and experience. The name that would have been used by their forebears is Koori but of late they are called Aboriginals, but irrespective, they are the First Australians.

In this land that Cai found himself, although called Australia, thousands of years ago it was part of the great Gondwana Land that was attached to Asia and encompassed most of the land mass of the Southern Hemisphere. For scientists, Gondwana Land is of interest because of the spread of organisms across the land bridges. For anthropologists, the interest is the flow of humanity from its roots in Southern Africa. For Cai, he was fascinated and never tired of learning about the land and its people. The Europeans came from every part of Europe, the United Kingdom and the Americas – all with their own funny accents and ways.

He was to learn about the "Bora", the time when an Aboriginal boy becomes a man. It is a time when their connection to the land is made and their responsibility to the land is felt. As their final act towards their initiation as an adult, they would go "walkabout". This would take many days, weeks or months. Usually they went on their own.

Before going, they were told, 'Before you were born your spirit existed in the form of an animal, a plant or as an ancestral spirit,

Continued

Cai shouted to the men, 'All wait, I go with him', and ran to catch up. And so, off they went.

Without taking you readers on that journey, it is enough to say that with the clever tracking skills and "knowing" of the land and its spirits, Gongshi had been located alive. It seemed that he had not been drinking his water, as he had been sharing it with those who were sicker than himself. In the night, he became disorientated and wandered off to find his Father and Mother. Once Cai gave him water, they lead him back to the camp where he made a full recovery.

It seems that their fortunes had also changed in that Jarri had seen one of those strange kan-ger-oos, and with stealth and cunning managed to spear it. Once cooked there was enough food to feed all the men. It was the first meat they had for weeks.

Cai felt at a disadvantage without knowing the Australian language, which was called English. To remedy this, several times a day he went to Chong the interpreter and asked him what this word was, or that word, in English. Chong had started to fear Cai but also respected this young leader and complied as he wanted to win his favour, if he could. Cai was quick to learn and each day added to his store of English words.

***

Good to his word, the guide returned on the evening of the fourth day. He had four other horses with him and another two aboriginal men who pulled the reigns of the two horses. When the men saw this small convoy, they cheered. The ancestors had heard them.

It was a happier camp that night.

***

When Cai went for his nightly visit with Jarri, one of the newly arrived Aboriginal men was with him. The other had gone back to Port Adelaide. The new man, like Jarri, had a smile that showed full acceptance. Cai, in time, was to grow to love these people, for their openness and acceptance of his Chinese comrades. The new man's name was Benny.

Benny could speak English and so Cai now had a method of understanding Jarri easier. Both were pleased.

Continued
and so as you go in search of manhood you search for your spirit. When you do this with intent, your story of the land is revealed. History is never far as it lives on in the land; it is your task to find that history. You will live off the land and respect all creatures, plants, shrubs and ancestor rocks. Listen to them, they will guide you. You will follow the song lines (dreaming tracks) of our ancestors by chanting the songs and hearing the call of the spirits. By singing you will bring the spirits and the land together, while finding the way of manhood. As part of your Bora, you have been taught chanting and things mystical. To go beyond the five senses where you enter The Dreamtime (time before conscious thought) and hear stories as told by the Ancestors. It is a time of solitude and reflection, and if you listen you will hear stories that come from our old culture.'

In 1889, in the town of Bendigo, police sergeant Henry Fred was given a solid gold medal for his kindness and good treatment of the Chinese citizens of the area. Inscribed (by hand) are the words … "he treated us as his own people." The medal now is housed in the Golden Dragon Museum of Bendigo.

Sitting at their fire they chatted. Cai asked Benny where he came from, and in the process learnt that in the land called Australia, before the Europeans arrived, Australia was made up of some one hundred and seventy eight separate Aboriginal nations (there is ongoing debate as to the exact number). Benny's country was down the south of South Australia as he was of the Bungandidj nation. Jarri was from the middle of the South Australian area, from the Parnkalla (later it was to become Barngarla) Country. Like all sovereign countries, they respected the laws and boundaries of each country. Listening carefully, he could detect that these two Aboriginals, from their own countries had rivalry between them. Although, they understood each other, they did have different dialects. To make it more interesting, they are both in this "country", which is the Yorta Yorta Nation, so both of them were trespassing, so to speak.

***

With the men having rested and things more settled, they were happy to leave at first light the next morning. It was an easy walk for the first session, and with their recovered strength, they seemed to be enjoying it. In the afternoon session, as they got deeper into the foothills of the mountain range, it became a more interesting landscape but physically more demanding.

As they started to collect the wood, before they were to stop, they heard the Guide's horse whinny. Drawing all their attention, they saw the horse rear high up in panic. The Guide, not expecting this was thrown off and landed on his head. He was dead before his feet hit the ground.

All gathered around in shock, but then there was a further commotion as Jarri, pushed through the crowd. He gestured for all to move back. Scanning the ground, he spoke to Cai via Benny. 'Snake… big brown snake… scare the horse.'

Cai well remembered the warning of impending doom that was to befall the Guide. *How did Jarri know this was to happen?* As he got to know more about the Aboriginals, he learnt that there was much that they saw or knew that most people did not.

***

Cai did not sleep much that night. As the men's designated leader, he had to plan what was best for them, now that they did not have the guide. Early the next morning he took his thoughts to Jarri and Benny, hoping they would help. With him, he dragged along Chong the interpreter.

The **bird life** of the Australian bush is prolific, with more varieties than most countries (nearly 900).

Kookaburra

Budgerigar (budgies)

Magpie

Parakeets (Photos curtesy of Pixabay)

Cai finally put his question to the Aboriginals. He needed to get the men to Bendigo, Dai Gum San. Neither knew the term Dai Gum San but Jarri knew of Bendigo – it is in Victoria, a very long way away. When Cai asked how far, Jarri could not answer in miles or kilometres as he knew of no such things. When he answered, he said maybe ten more days, maybe twelve. Better fourteen because Chinamen are not good for walking, they too slow, not strong, so must have rest days.

Then the big question that Cai had considered earlier, 'Can you take us?... Will you take us?... I am sure we could find some money to pay you... you both, because Benny you must also come, to help with translation.'

The men were perplexed, they had never been asked such a thing, and broke out in their own language. Whilst they were talking, Cai was amused that this three-way language discussion with four different dialects was working. When they were ready to talk, their first question was, 'What do we do with Mr. Guide?... bad business that one.' Cai wanted to ask how Jarri knew this was going to happen but put the thought aside as this was more important business.

Instead, he said, 'I'm thinking this Mr. Benny leaves straight away, with Mr. Guide on his horse. He can explain what happened, and explain what we are doing. Then... if you agree... we leave in an hour. But Mr. Benny must come back and find us. I am sure he can because there are lots of feet to follow, and I can see that you could track an ant which leave no footprints.' All four men laughed at the description of their tracking ability.

So that is what happened, Benny left with the body of the Guide on his horse, Jarri agreed to take them to Bendigo, and Chong moaned that he had no real choice, but once Cai reminded him that he probably was still getting a wage from the merchants, he must accept it.

***

Once it became too dark to continue they settled down on a hillock that overlooked a valley of trees. The ever-present mountains outlined the rim of Cai's view.

Weary from his day, it did not take Cai long to fall asleep but later, damp from the heavy dew, he woke up cold. The full moon gave luminance to the sky so bright, few stars were visible. The mountains and trees were a dark form against the lighter sky. He woke again and saw that the moon had shifted its position far to the west. Still too early to get up he slept some more.

Koala Bears

We all love these sleepy creatures with their cute faces, the large, round ears, and the big button noses. In addition, not having the tail adds to the fun. They only live in certain gum trees, and only eat the leaves of those specific varieties. Because of their limited diet, they are sedentary and sleep about twenty hours a day. They carry their babies in a pouch, much like the kangaroo as mentioned above. They are a close species of the kangaroo.

Koala fully grown

Mother and child (Photos curtesy of Pixabay)

At dawn, he shivered with the cold. A few birds chirped as they set about their day.

To his right a slither of light grew and clawed its way to prominence. Attached, as if by a long rope, was the sun that gave colour and form to the valley below and a distant mountain. As the rope dragged the sun higher, more colour was added until individual trees and rocks could be seen.

He watched all of this with wonder. The birds, an orchestra, increased its tempo and song. When the sun finally rolled its nose over the horizon, slithers of light stretched across the land and inserted shadows into crevices on the trees and rocks. Suddenly, the sun was fully developed, big, round and bright. The yellow warmth fed into him. He realised they were running late, and so he was keen for them to get going as it was likely to be hot later.

***

Progress was good, the men more settled and relationships were forged. It took another two days to cross the mountain range. The land on the other side was flat, dry sand. A desert. The days were even hotter. They came to a large river, mighty in its length (2,500 kilometres) and width, which later was to be known as the Murray River, or the Murray for short. The Murray was the border between South Australia and Victoria, and posed a problem as to how to get a across.

Up to this point in time, the only people they saw were those tribe's people on their second day of journeying. There were some rough tracks going to the Victorian border, which they felt it wiser to not travel in case there were Victorian border patrols.

Jarri felt this was a good place to rest for a day. The men could wash and relax. He warned that they must not go deeper than their knees because the river was strong and could wash them away. He said to Cai that, 'He go and give respect to "this country's" people, and ask how we can get across.'

When Cai asked, 'How will you find them?' Jarri chuckled.

'They find me… they already know we here.' Nevertheless, he seemed to know which way to go and with determined steps it was not long before he, along with the dingo were found.

Snakes

Australia has at least ten poisonous snakes, that can kill within a short period of time after sustaining a bite. Some of these are: the red-bellied black snake, death adder, mulga snake, taipan, king brown snake, tiger snake, copperhead, broad head snake.

It was only a month ago that there was an item on the news where a father was trying to protect his young toddler from a King Brown snake that had somehow got into the bathroom of the farmhouse. The snake bit the father – two hours later, he was dead.

Eastern Brown (Photos curtesy of Wikipedia Commons)

Tiger snake

Half a day later, he returned, this time with four tribesmen and a youth. It seemed that they were mollified that Jarri had gone to them to ask permission to cross their country. They lived on the banks of the river and survived from hunting the land and fishing in the river. It also seemed that they wanted to see the Chinamen for themselves, and pulled the outer skin of their eyes in mimicking the Chinese faces. All laughed. They explained that on the other side of the river was another country – Victoria.

Jarri said, 'Down the river, about half a day's walk, there are a series of sand banks.' Because it was the dryer season, the river was lower and so they could wade across. They would do this the next day.

As tradition would have it, a fire was made and the seven black men sat around it and told stories. The visitors left the next morning.

***

The crossing was made without issue and further into the desert they walked. Even though they replenished their water from the river, all the men complained that the water was too little. Thinking about this, it occurred to Cai that Jarri had not carried water, and so he asked him where he is getting his water. 'From the ground, where else?' as if this was a stupid question.

'Can you show us how to find water?'

'No… you not bush clever. But I can show you where water is', and he did. Still they had to use it sparingly, often it was several days between water points. From this, Fuju made a suggestion. At each water hole, they could make a sign in their own language for any other Chinese people who were forced to follow their path. That way they would know where water was. The suggestion was adopted and became a regular occurrence from that time onwards, where all water holes were marked in Chinese script.

Every two days or so, either Jarri or Benny, would go off on his own. When they came back, usually it was with a kangaroo over a shoulder. The men cheered as they were developing a taste for this meat, especially cooked in the Aboriginal way; tossing the entire carcass on the hot coals and letting it cook through the fur and skin. When ready, the fur was easy to remove. The men had now seen many kangaroos and as they ate the meat, they kept pretending to jump.

Emus are flightless birds who roam the terrain on long legs that power them up to great speeds and for long periods at a time. With their tall necks, they reach two metres high, they are the largest bird of this massive land. Resident for many thousands of years and perfectly adapted to the harsh and unpredictable conditions, they can go weeks without food and days without water.

A name that has acceptance by the First Nation's people of Australia is that of the "Traditional Owners" of the land. They would never say owners themselves, they were (and still should be) the "Traditional Caretakers/Custodians" of the land.

Fully grow emu (curtesy of Pixabay)

There were other kills such as snakes and a strange looking bird called an emu. Emus were taller than the largest of the men. The meat was also to their liking. At one time Benny returned with an emu and three emu eggs. They were big eggs and each would feed two or three men, but these three were more to give the men a taste. One man asked could he have gotten more eggs. Benny replied, 'Yes, but we never take all. We want some to hatch so there are always enough emus.'

On about the twelfth day, they came across the bodies of eight Chinese people. Luckily, there was a ninth man, who was alive – just. After water, food, and some herbs that Benny dug up, the man recovered and travelled with them. He told the men that they paid a full fare to come to Australia, as by not going through merchants, it cost less. All the people in his village helped pay his way so he can bring riches and honour to all of them. They did not have the money enough to pay the ten-pound tax to enter Victoria. He was told it was only two days walk to the gold fields, at a place called Ballarat. When he saw that two Aboriginals were leading them, he panicked and was told that three Aboriginals had been contracted to guide them.

They had to pay the money upfront, before they left. Then for two days, they took them and they trusted them. When we woke up on the third morning, they were gone. 'They also took some of our food.' He was too emotional to continue and had to be helped to calm down. Later he said, 'Bad people these… they also run away… they yeman ren.' Cai felt that, certainly, Jarri could be trusted, he had spent too many nights at his campfire. He tried to assure the man. He reminded them that neither Benny nor Cai, had asked for money. It seemed that they were doing this because a bunch of Chinamen got themselves into difficulty.

Once they were deeper into Victoria there were more hills and trees. As a farmer, Cai reasoned that *if there was more water, this land could be productive*. That always led him to think of his father and mother. He knew he would honour them.

It was still very hot through the days. All along the way, Jarri went to ask permission of the local tribe's people to cross and respect their land. Never were they aggressive and always helped. Occasionally, they came across some who told Cai that they must not stay on their land and not to go to any sacred areas. Cai always respected the request and so they hurried across those parts of that country. Within each meeting, Jarri would ask for guidance and direction, where water was and plenty of meat to hunt.

After one such discussion, Benny reported that they should be at "their Bendigo" in two days. The men cheered.

***

Not only was Cai becoming proficient in English, he was picking up Aboriginal words. Benny helped him to learn a kind of a generic language that many of the Aboriginal used across different nations.

Listening to them talk about their beliefs of the spirits and the land, how the land was wise, he was struck with the similarity to the Taoism from his country… everything must be in balance, Ying with Yang, and that there is an absolute principle that balances the entire universe and all things. From this, a method or code must be followed to achieve the natural order and harmony. All ill health and bad luck can be attributed to being out of this balance. Like the "Aboriginal Lore", there is only one truth, and that truth cannot be seen. Both tell that you cannot separate man from the land, or from the trees, the rivers – everything affects everything. It is accepting that what we do or think has an effect on everything else.

Within Cai's village at home, most practiced the Tao and consequently there was little crime or fighting. Jarri and Benny taught him that although they had a country, they did not own it, they were only the custodians. They must pass the land on to the next generation in "proper" condition. Another similarity is what he heard earlier of their Miwe, because in the Tao, listening to your gut, your intuition or that that is within you is important.

On the long walks, Cai had plenty of time to think through issues…

These Aborigines seem to be an ancient people. They have had thousands of years to understand these principles, and more importantly, if the principles work. The same with Taoism, going back so far no one really knows when it started. Tao means the way, which is the truth to respect the land, spirits, the ancestors, and other people and so it is to respect ourselves.

Within this last statement, Cai developed and lived his own set of ideals, and as the reader continues this story, you will see that many of the behaviours that Cai exhibited were a result of this structure.

***

As they got closer to Bendigo town, they started to come across more people, some black, most white. They also came upon a few Chinese people all with different dialects. When they chatted to these people, they learnt that, 'You think it was hard getting here, it's harder working, like a worm deep in the ground.' There were stories of death, of poverty, and seldom were there riches. Most though did earn money and to put it to good use.

Cai thought it a good idea to set up camp at the edge of the town and then asked Fuju and Chong the interpreter to go in to the town to find the merchants. When they returned, they said the merchants would come tomorrow in the morning. They also had stories to tell of 'a thousand holes, where people dug for gold... very dangerous, not good.' There were also people looking for gold in the creeks that they passed. But also bad opium houses, full of people, and places called pubs where many were drunk and it looked like they had been drunk for long time.

***

The merchants were not happy to hear that the guide was dead. Nor were they happy to know that the men had a spokesperson. At first when they saw that it was Cai, who by then had turned thirteen, and grown an inch in height, they thought that he would be easy to deal with but they soon learned otherwise. Through the discussion, Cai was able to secure a good wage for Jarri and Benny for bringing them safely to Bendigo. He also chastised the merchants for being greedy and the way they were treated on the ship and not having enough food for the big walk. This was said with all of the men listening and there were many cries of, 'There was not enough food, and the food was rotten and you lied to us, and lied and lied.'

Cai also informed them that he was going to send a letter back to his homeland warning any others as to how his men have been treated. He would not do that because by doing so it would bring sadness upon his parents and relatives and all the parents and relatives of all of the men. The men had previously discussed this and this was the decision that they made. Nevertheless, these greedy merchants needed to be told that so hopefully things would improve from there on in for the others that followed.

***

Those who were well enough started work the next day. They were allocated work at various diggings, all owned or operated by white people. The work was hard and dirty, from sun up to sun set, six days a week.

It would seem that Cai had been allocated to one of the most dangerous mines, probably on purpose by the merchants. Still, Cai did not complain and put his back into the work. Some of the mines produced less gold than the others and that was the case with Cai's mine. With the little income, after receiving his half pay, he was most prudent and saved his money in the Chinese cartel bank.

I will not spend much time on Cai's gold mining time, other than this short overview.

At the time, Cai, and the men arrived, Bendigo was in the grip of "gold fever" and nothing was normal. It had at this time more gold mined there than anywhere else in the world. And it wasn't only Chinese people who came, so did people from many parts of the world. It was an exciting time, and for most people their life was already a time of hardship and poverty, and so the lure and excitement of gold saw them come in their thousands. Many were thieves, rascals and scoundrels. But many were honest and hard working, people who just wanted a break in life. Whenever you have an unbalanced society, which this was, of ninety-seven percent men, and a place of little or biased law, there will always be extream societies of prostitutes and people of the church trying to save souls.

The Chinese community, which was now much larger than just Cai's members, were for the most part hard-working and industrious. They were determined to make good of their time, to honour their parents, and to make a life for themselves – and most did.

The easy gold, which was the alluvial gold, had ended by the time Cai's group arrived. So it was the difficult and dangerous deep-shaft mines they worked in, of which there were over 5,000 in the area.

The dangerous shaft that the merchants put Cai into was 900 metres deep (remember this was in the 1850s). He had lost at least a dozen friends who had been killed from rock falls or collapses. At one stage he was lucky as a large rock dislodged from above, and as it soundlessly fell, it grazed the outside of his right shoulder. If it was a match stick closer to his head he would have been killed or at least crippled.

There were times when it was almost as dangerous out of the mine as in it – as there were clashes and fighting amongst the races. Almost weekly Cai was asked to try and intervene and be a mediator on behalf of his Chinese countrymen. Sometimes he was successful and at other times he wasn't – but irrespective, he gained a reputation as being astute and fair to both sides. There were even times that he was asked to mediate between owners and their European workers.

Cai also did not squander his free time. After he had learnt to speak basic English, he went to the Chinese Community School that has been set up to teach those who wanted to learn to read and write English. He went to this after-hours four days a week.

After the two years, his commitment to the merchants were over. He had reasonable skills in speaking, reading, and writing English – he felt that these were an imperative if he was going to make his fortune.

Another activity that occupied any free time that he may have had was to look at the land on the outskirts of Bendigo, where there was water and also tracks into the town. Upon completing his first morning working's work in the mine, he knew that he was not going to do that for one day longer than necessary. He could see that there was a shortage of good Chinese food for the masses of Chinese men who worked the mines and supportive industries. He knew that food was their blood and the lack of decent Chinese food was almost as disheartening as not being able to have a Chinese wife with them. It was his intention to put a deposit down on some acres and create a market garden, which focused on Chinese produce. He felt that by growing these, and selling them directly to the Chinese community that he would break into the market faster.

He asked Fuju if he would be a partner in this business. At the time he said, 'Fuju, you are better than a brother, you joined our blood together on the ship that bought us here. We have been side by side ever since, we must do this together… together we will honour our families with wealth…'

Benny and Jarri had remained in the Bendigo minefield area, where they took up any odd jobs that they could find. Benny had found romance with a girl from the local indigenous community, and a child was on the way. Jarri stayed, as he wanted to be with Cai. They could have worked in the mines but they were against that, saying they may be black like ants but ants live underground and that was not for them. When Cai asked them if they wanted to work for him, they jumped at the opportunity. They knew nothing of gardening and were not overly interested in that either. But they did other jobs around the land, such as building shacks to live in, sheds for storage and work areas and under the supervision of Cai, they also helped to do a lot of the trenching for irrigation. Before the irrigation came, Cai and Fuju carried the water for the produce from the creek that passed at the border of the land. They each carried two buckets attached to a stick that sat across their shoulders. Literally thousands of times they walked down the steep sides to the creek and then carried the heavy buckets back up the hill and over to the land.

Australian Spiders
There are around 2,900 varieties. Of the venomous varieties, the most common is the Redback spider. In fact, when a young man I was bitten by one on the foot. Within an hour the bite was an angry red and extremely itchy. Four hours later, the swelling started. The next morning the foot was so swollen I could not put on a shoe, the pain intense. I was nauseaus with a headache. For three days I could not go to work. Within a week I had made a full recovery. As I said I was a young man and full of health. However, if I was older and with less vitality, I could have died.

The funnel-web spider is potentially fatal if not treated quickly.

Red-Back spider courtesy of Pixaby

According to the National Museum of Australia, in 1857, 40% of the men of Bendigo were Chinese.

In the early days of the mining, the Chinese were far more efficient than the Westerners. They sorted themselves into teams or a collective, where different functions were to support the overall endeavor.

For instance, some were cooks, so that when breaks were had, the food was ready. Some grew vegetables. The kitchen therefore, was communal. Others built the shacks or buildings that supported the community.

Whereas, the Europeans worked in groups of about five people, but when they finished in the mine for the day, they fended for themselves.

The Chinese miners, therefore could work longer hours in the mine. All proceeds gained were shared by all who contributed.

It was only later that the Europeans got better organized, but this was as a result of funding that came in via corporations.

Cai and Fuju had pretty much spent most of their money to secure a deposit for the land and had no wages to pay the two aboriginal men. By this time, Jarri and Benny had grown to love and respect the two Chinese men. They were prepared to work for them until money came in from the first crops. Having run out of money, Cai and Fuju needed some for tools and equipment, seeds for planting and not to mention food to live on. Of course, to start with, the white owned banks were seldom prepared to lend Chinese people money, but they did get limited funds from Chinese moneylenders.

So after two years of living in the area, and having proven himself to be honest, hard-working and sober, and a non-taker of opium, people in the area, both Chinese and whites, started to trust Cai.

Along with his Taoist beliefs, which was simplicity, Cai wanted a simplistic name for their fledgling enterprise, and simply called it Shandong Market Garden with a symbol of the Chinese peasant-farmer's conical straw hat with the wide brim to protect from the sun. He specifically used the term market garden in English as opposed to Chinese text because he knew that in time if he was to grow their enterprise that he would need working relationships with white businessmen.

As Benny and Jarri were not from that country, Cai asked of them to make contact with the local tribespeople from whose "country" the land was in, and ask them if they would come and give permission for them to work the land, with respect. Jarri further suggested they ask them to do a ceremony on the land and asked for the blessing of their ancestors.

The day of the ceremony started off cold and rainy. However, as if the land was ready to be blessed, the sun came out, bringing its warmth. The local tribe's people (The Dja dja Wurrung) asked for blessings.

Fong, the man who took on the priestly duties for the men was on hand to also ask the ancestors to bless the land. Joss sticks lit, and drums were banged. A small six-man dragon had been borrowed and paraded and ran this way and that way, all around the sacred fire – this was to the amusement of the indigenous people.

Adding to the amazement of the indigenous people was when Cai spoke. At first, he greeted everybody in English, then in his native dialect of Chinese, then using the generic indigenous language that Benny had taught him, welcomed everybody in their language. He wove his speech with all three languages, he spoke of their connection between all people, and the land. He spoke of how Shandong Market Garden would be run with respect for the land, and the people who lived and worked on it.

The indigenous people were delighted with the fact that Cao could speak to them in an indigenous language that they understood and with words of love and respect for the land. The whites who had been invited, or who came out of interest, thought it was all mumbo-jumbo and that the only governing factor of whether the land would grow and prosper was the expertise of the farmer, and of course luck with the climate. Later, after the ceremonies, a party was had with many toasts, and cheers, and ganbei(ing), where the white people tried to convince the indigenous and Chinese people of the folly of partnership with ancestors and respecting the land. Neither the indigenous elders or Cai and Fuju bothered to try and convince the whites otherwise. For the indigenous people and the Chinese people, the knowing looks between them was enough. They knew of the way of things and that had no need to convince these white people. Generally, those white people were friendly and helpful and were happy that Shandong Market Garden would grow into a successful business. They were also interested in following the progress over the following months and years to see if it was going to be successful.

It was in their second year of production, whereby some white farmers and merchants tried to shut down the Shandong Market Garden as it was taking too much business away from them. Coinciding with this, there were a few acts of sabotage on the farm. The culprits were easily confronted because of the tracking abilities of Jarri. The culprits were indeed shocked when this aboriginal man, accompanied by his growling dingo, and some fifty Chinese men banged on their door. These culprits were easily persuaded to reveal the business people who had paid them to sabotage.

When the rest of the Chinese community heard about these efforts to shut Shandong Market Garden down, they threatened not to buy from those same farmers and merchants. From that time onwards, there were no more problems for Shandong Market Garden.

Shandong Market Garden expanded to the point where they had paid back all loans, including paying Jarri and Benny. Cai and Fuju were able to purchase additional land on the other side of the creek. Their produce spread beyond vegetables, also including pigs, chickens and ducks, and some beef followed. Seemingly, the local population could not get enough of the Shandong Market Garden produce.

Next, they grew rice. The only rice at the time had been imported from China. It was old, full of weevils, and expensive. At one stage, on a trip back to China, Cai went and learnt how it was done in areas where there was not that much water, and so Shandong Market Garden utilised these methods with moderate success without consuming too much water. This went well for many years, until the Victorian Government allocated large tracts of land next to the Murray River, near Swan Hill for large companies to grow rice. Cai and Fuku, by then were old men, and it did not matter, but rice had played a part in their company growth.

Fuju also planted a pomelo tree after his first visit back home. A kind of citrus tree, native to South-East Asia, which grows a large yellow fruit with sweet white flesh. This is sometimes called Chinese grapefruit. The Mandarin word for pomelo (yòuzi) and also means "blessing" because the fruit is considered auspicious. The tree, or rather the branches and leaves, were also used to start the celebrations of the lunar period of the Chinese New Year.

Shandong Market Garden, which had now grown into a large enterprise, invested with others including Chinese restaurants, which became popular with the Chinese community. In time though, the whites started to eat in them and developed a taste for the foods that have been satisfying the pallets of the Chinese for hundreds of years. They loved the clean tastes of the crisp vegetables, the rice, the meat and the carefully selected spices that brought the meal together, though there were many foods that the whites avoided and recoiled against, such as the intestine of duck or fish eyes. It was partly because of the use of "very different" animal parts that some of these whites were happy to regard the Chinese as heathens, and subhuman beings.

The friendship and cooperation between Shandong Market Garden and the local indigenous people grew, a camaraderie that was forged as both races were on the wrong end of racial contempt. The Aboriginals were not considered people with regards to the various colonial constitutions, or later the Australian Government constitution. They were represented in the constitutions as animal and flora (bush, flowers), and the Chinese were not liked because they took jobs away from the white Australians. Those white Australians (and still a few today) feared the Chinese because they did not bother to take the time to get to know them as people. Those are and were narrow minded views.

The managers of Shandong Market Garden encouraged friendship with the local black community. The Aboriginals, in turn, accepted that friendship, where both cultures found respect. Of course, there were individuals on both sides who were non-accepting of the other race.

In the early days of Shandong Market Garden, although Benny and Jarri were not farmers, they taught Cai and Fuju much about the Australian bush and landscape. They in turn were able to include this knowledge in day-to-day farm management. For instance, they were taught that the bark of some species of gum trees was good as a mulch to cover a garden bed to stop moisture evaporation from the blazing sun. They also made rope from the bark of a tree and mats from which to line walkways. The best nutrient for the gardens that

Danger from the Sea

Australia is famous for its shark attacks, which are often fatal or sever limbs. There are other terrors from the Australian sea that can kill or make one very ill if stung or bitten.

The Blue Ringed Octopus resides in rock pools on the coast. Radiating changing iridescent blue circles, and the fact that they are small (about 50mm in diameter) means that they attract interest. People pick them up and place them in the palm of their hand, fascinated – whilst the octopus sinks its proboscis into the skin of the palm, thereby injecting its venom. First paralysis, and within a few hours, the person may be dead. One report said that one blue ringed octopus has enough venom in it to kill twenty-six adults.

The Box Jellyfish

The venom of some species of box jellyfish is extremely potent and is considered by many as the most venomous creature on earth. Their stings are agony and can be deadly to humans. The jellyfish, which moves quickly through the water, collides with the human who is swimming or splashing in its path. Small filaments carry the venom and cardiac arrest can happen within two to three minutes. Treatment is simple; apply vinegar as soon as the victim comes out of the water. The patient will also require hospitalisation. They are not indigenous to Australia and are in the tropical waters of other parts of the world where they traverse via the trade winds and currents.

The Stone Fish

When seen underwater, it looks just like a stone. Usually unseen until threatened, it reveals a series of spikes which contain venom. When stood on, the venom shoots into the foot of the person. Like the jellyfish, there is great pain and death can follow quickly, by cardiac arrest. If treated quickly a full recovery will happen but it can take many weeks for the pain to subside.

That is enough of the dangers of the sea for you because if you visit Australia, you may never want to go into our wonderful waters!

The Blue Ringed Octopus
By Jens Petersen - Own work, CC BY 2.5, https://commons.wikimedia.org/w/index.php?curid=1430987

they could use was to collect the small round pellets (poo) from the kangaroos that populated the area then soak these in water. Two or three days later they would pour the water on the garden beds where the produce doubled in size. These practices were kept a close secret and the white farmers could never work out how produce that came from Shandong Market Garden was always bigger, healthier, and tastier than their own.

The Chinese also gave the indigenous people great skills in things like farming, as many of the indigenous people started their own small gardens to help feed their family. They also taught them animal husbandry.

Over the years, they saw children being born into the indigenous communities and watched those children grow up. Each culture was eager to help the other. It was not good that the whites ostracised both communities, but it did help to bring these communities together to forge strong bonds.

It was around this time that Cai really became the statesman and advocate for the people. This was not just for Chinese people but all people because he did not see colour or race – he only saw people.

On one such occasion he had been called to a riot because the government of Victoria had yet again, levied another tax against Chinese people. This, apparently was to limit the growth of the Chinese population. It was outside the Bendigo Town Hall where a meeting of the local counsellors was being held. About eighteen Chinese men gathered and demanded to go into the hall to see these counsellors. A line of policeman barred their entry. The Chinese men were pushing and shoving, and as they did they shouted the words, 'Why this tax on Chinamen? Chinamen work very hard but get little money, we pay all the other taxes, we can't pay more tax. Why difference made between Chinamen and other men? We obey law, we good citizens, we want be friends with Englishmen – why we not let be so? We no trouble to Government or the police? We go to jail before we pay 'nother tax.'

Cai was able to calm the crowd down because he received acknowledgement from some of the councilors that when they broke for lunch, they would come and hear what the men said, which is exactly what they did. They promised they would take the requests to the Parliament in Melbourne.

***

It was sixteen long years before Cai was able to go home. He had sent money when he could and even bought out to Australia his Number Four Brother. His return was grander than when he left. This time he

Fatalities from Australian Wildlife
Above I have given information on some of the dangers that lurk in the Australian bush or waters. Yet, for all of these combined dangers there are probably fewer than fifty deaths a year. For instance, most snakes will slither away when they feel the vibration of someone walking (although not always – the Tiger Snake will not only stand its ground, it will often rush at the walker). With spiders, when camping, caution is taken with zip up tents or houses are screened and regularly cleaned to eliminate them. With the sea animals, it is known not to walk in water in the tropics without shoes on where Stone Fish are. The information on the Blue Ringed Octopus is well known by most Australians. Of course, sharks bring terror to the heart of all, so they are avoided.

Should you ever come to these shores, learn of the dangers and be safe.

The *Argus (newspaper)*, 11 April 1864
One very remarkable feature in the vegetable exhibits (referring to an annual country fair) was that a Chinaman of Spring Creek, named Chin Queen, (who) carried off six or seven prizes... While the European Gardens have been thoroughly desiccated (at this dry time), this industrious individual has maintained a succession of crops by irrigation. Water and manure are the two secrets – if such a can be called – of a horticultural success of our celestial visitors. Every day these patient and laborious individuals may be seen carrying off in (their) baskets the refuse of the hotel stable.

Reported on 3 January 1865, The Argus *(newspaper) when referring to farming*
That instead of placing all the manure underneath the soil (as we English do), the Chinese spread a portion of it on the surface with the seed beneath, and the effect of the large surface watering is that a liquid manure is carried down, while the straw of the manure protects the soil from the sun... The growth, under the care of these people, is amazingly rapid – a consequence of which is that many of the articles (produce) grown are succulent and tender, and there is not time for blight (rot or infection) to attack them... Barefooted, at a smart trot, the men bring up about 1000 buckets (of water) per day, which they pour on the plants. It will be remembered that, according to English notions of gardening, water can only be safely applied between sundown and sunrise. The Chinese water three times a day – once during the heat of

Continued

had employed his own carriage – he needed to as he had so many presents for his parents and his siblings. He would never see his grandmother or grandfather again as both of them had passed on. As he approached the village, he had mixed feelings. Knowing he would see his siblings and his parents warmed his heart with happiness, but when he thought of his grandparents, his heart broke. As he approached the village, he could see a crowd waiting. It was as if there was a festival, and indeed the feeling was festival-like. As he got closer, the young ones of the village could not wait until the carriage got to him they ran to meet him. Cai was also too impatient and jumped off the moving wagon, as he ran towards them.

As he rushed towards the main gate, surrounded by all the laughing children, all jumping up and down with joy he remembered the harshness of the place and the climate and how difficult life was here. Some of the older people were no longer there but new little ones were running around.

As he got to the gate there were many people who shook his hand and welcomed him, some slapped his back, all laughed and were happy in the moment, as if a savior had arrived. That was how they all saw Cai – a savior, because of the money he had sent back for his parents. The money did not only stay with the parents, a lot of it went out to the community to help others in desperate need. Suddenly, his mother stepped in front of him, with tears of joy she grabbed him and held him tight. She could not stop saying, 'My Number One son... My Number One son... You are home, you are home.'

His father's face then loomed in front of him. His normal reserved demeanour had given way to the love and happiness that he felt for his eldest son. He also grabbed and hugged Cai, where the three embraced with tears of joy glistening down their cheeks.

He did not know how long they stood embracing but they came back to earth when Mother said, 'Come there is food for you.' He knew all his favourites would be there waiting, and upon entering the house, he had never seen so much food in there at any other time. All the village contributed to this special return feast.

Inside the house everybody wanted to speak to him, to touch his arm, to smile at him. Some of the older ladies of the village took his face in their hands and scrutinised the lines, the wrinkles, his eyes to see if, still, that gentleness that they remembered was there. He was now a man and it was obvious that his experiences in the harshness of life would be drawn in his face, but they could see that the boy who went away was still the same person who stood before them – that was what they wanted to see. They did not want to see a man who had returned broken by life. Nor did they want to see one who came back who was too interested in money or power. They left the house with joy in their hearts.

Continued

the sun. It is no doubt the frequent and consistency of the watering which renders this a safe and successful system. Neglect in preserving the moisture would be fatal... Another distinction observable is the remarkable closeness of planting. This is not done to economise ground, but chiefly to save labour in watering, as well as to make the plants themselves protect the soil from the sun. The lettuce, for instance, are sown with the onions, and removed in sufficient time not to interfere with them. Where the lettuces are planted by themselves they are not placed more than four or five inches apart or about 16 to 1 grown in an equal area used by the English gardeners. The consequence is that they form a dense mass – the ground not being visible at all – and apparently from their pressure on each other, the heart (of the lettuce) is soon formed, and they have a tendency to grow tall. In using the liquid manure, great care is taken to not touch the plants, and manure and water are used on alternate days. In one example, the soil adjoining the dam is of the most sterile quality, being formed of that species of hard, clean gravel so opposed to vegetation, and which before being broken up was as bare and beaten looking as a public road. About a month ago two Chinamen thought the area a pleasant one, and accordingly a large plot was laid out... It may now be observed, one of the finest and greenest crops of Chinese cabbage and French beans to be found in the district.

Also from the *Argus (newspaper)*, 14 July 1866

There is no variety in their style, one sample may be taken as a model for all Chinese gardens throughout the colony. The long rows of uneven, well manured, well watered beds meet the eye in all cases... Their mode is in many respects very different to that followed by our English gardeners. They force the vegetation of all plants by loading the beds with manure, keeping the ground well watered, and nearly always selecting a situation where the sun has full play on the ground. In summer the vegetables are not dried up in the same way as they are in other gardens (European) but grow at a prodigious rate. This may be accounted for by the fact that the ground is always kept perfectly saturated with water. The long irregular rows of beds are entirely free from weeds, being turned over too frequently to allow any wild vegetation to make headway. The vegetables produced by the Chinese are fresh and tender. Frequently the market would be entirely without a supply would it not be for these industrious people.

As much as he wanted to eat all that beautiful foods, he was too excited, too unsettled, and so even though the house was full of people he said to his Number Two Brother, 'Come, walk with me… let's go to the fields.'

There was no change, things were exactly the same as they were in his time there. There were however more modern tools and implements that made the work easier. These came from the money that he had sent. Seeing all this made him realise how much that decision that he had made on the boat to fend for himself and be responsible for himself – how much that had supported him in his growth, and just how important it was. He was still a young man with many years in front of him and although it had been hard, he was glad that his father had forced it on him.

When back at the house and all the villagers had gone, and it was just him and his family, it was a very special time for him. His father took him outside to chat about many things. He was gray and his body not upright anymore, stooped with thousands of hours out in the field. They talked about that day that he left on the wagon with the other children and his father said, 'It nearly broke our hearts to see you go. I knew you would survive…I knew you were strong. And now I see you in front of me, a man… a successful man… you make me very proud my son.' They embraced again and Cai thanked his father for making that decision. 'At the time I was angry with you for sending me away from you and Mother and my family. I can see it was the right way at the time and if I have bought money and honour to you and my family, in it brings me the greatest joy.'

***

His time there was only a month as he had to get back to help with the planting for the new season before the rains came. As his arrival there was so joyous, his departure was so sad. He had grown to love the country that now supported him and many of its people, but there is something about his heritage and his home that was deeply embedded, like legs are a part of the body. Now, he had another reason to be even sadder, for he had found love. It was not his intention to do so but when Hao came into the house after many of the villages had left on his first day back, it only took one look at her and his heart was her heart. She had been part of his childhood and came from six houses up the dirt track. She was four years younger than him, and when in Australia he had often thought of her with fondness, but as the eight-year-old girl that she was at the time. It never occurred to him that she could have grown into a woman, a beautiful woman. He could see that she was respectful to the elders and she knew when to be quite and not to interrupt. She was gentle with the children, even though they were running around like mad things because of the festival atmosphere. She had come to pay her respects and even wondered if he would remember her.

Today, pretty much all Australians love Chinese food and it fits very well within the culinary delights brought to Australia by all of the immigrants from the many different countries. So when one walks down the street of any city in Australia, there will be Chinese, Italian, Thai, Japanese, Greek and many others cultural restaurants to entice.

The *Argus*, 14 July 1866
However, altogether the Chinese gardener is a very useful to the colonist, and a great acquisition to large community requiring vegetables... If the settlement on the land of a number of industrious and skilled agriculturalists could be secured, a great boon would be conferred on the colony; for in addition to our own knowledge, that of a people who have cultivated and tilled in a warmer climate for thousands of years would be most important.

As a point of interest, even now, in 2018, the First Australians are still not fully recognised in the Australian constitution, nor in many of the state constitutions – but this is not the fault of the Australian population as a whole, as most (now) want indigenous recognition and inclusion. It is the Federal Government that does not have the will or courage to move down this path of what is right. Of course, this causes much resentment for the First Australian people.

The current Aboriginal population in Australia is just over half a million people, making up just 2.8 percent of the population. This is less than the Chinese population.

Another tax that the Victorian Government levied was a gold mining licence. The cost was twenty seven pounds, twelve shillings a year. This was a small fortune in those days. If a miner was found working without a licence, he was sentenced to a term in jail. However, the Eureka Rebellion in 1854 saw the fee drop to one pound a year.

This rebellion was not only about the licences, it was against the harsh working conditions that all the miners endured, and although the troops put the rebellion down with twenty-seven deaths and many jail sentences, the rebellion did manage to gain public support and sympathy for the miners.

Most of those rebelling were from The United Kingdom. There were some Chinese who also rebelled. I could not get any further information on the Chinese workers' involvement.

Before he finally left, she was the one who he said his last goodbyes to, and it was simple. As he looked into her eyes, he asked her if she would wait for him. She said, 'I have been waiting since I was eight years old… a few more years won't make any difference.' She asked him if he wanted to find more gold.

'No,' he said. 'S'pose I find gold, and I get rich… or it's gone tomorrow… could be with it I get lots pretty women… no, I want you as my wife, your children.' He told her that he wasn't quite ready to have her with him in Australia, as he wanted to build a better house and to make it better for her. The government there was starting to bow to the pressure from the Chinese men of allowing their women to come to them. So hopefully, in a few years' time he would be able to come and get her.

He did, as soon as he could. Together they made the house a home, filled with three happy children. It was a home of laughter, the smell of food cooking and where lots of friends visited.

***

Years later, the various enterprises were being run by his family, or people who he could trust. Many were white as things had changed in Australia and it was much easier for the Chinese people. Many were also Aboriginal and some were children who had been born when he first got there.

Cai still kept an eye on things but had plenty of time to pursue other endeavours. Always the supporter of the poor and the racially discriminated against, he worked tirelessly in lobbying the government for various causes. He set up or supported organisations that fought for fairness and justice for all. He was on the board of at least a dozen different charities and organisations. At least weekly, he would be asked to give a speech or a lecture here or there, and most of the time his theme was the same, but the stories around them differed, and although he never mentioned his Taoist beliefs, his message was around compassion and gentleness, balance in life, that fairness be given to all. He would tell them that he was not here for himself… he was here for the people, after all, he would say to the audience, 'Without people, we are nothing.'

His audience would say things like, 'You must be very clever, making yourself so rich and successful.'

'No,' he would say, and in humility tell them, 'I have just been very lucky.'

When Fuju and Cai were too involved in other areas of business, not only within the Bendigo region, but also other parts of Australia, to and from China, their children took over the active running of Shandong Market Garden. This continued for many years until finally Shandong Market Garden was purchased by one of the multinational farming companies and was absorbed into their mega billion-dollar businesses. Both men made many trips back to China to reconnect with their families, and the land on which they grew up. When they did travel back, always they took their families back with them because they wanted their children to be as Chinese as they were Australian. Both Benny and Jarri, were white haired, and spent their time with their grandchildren.

***

The lineage of Cai continues with two hundred and thirty descendants to carry his genes and his heritage. From his children, and his children's children, and his grandchildren's children, today they are in all a strata of life. Some are in business, there are nurses and doctors, builders and plumbers. There are computer programmers and IT specialists. There are house mothers and happy grandmothers to look after the children. There are smiling grandfathers who sit in the sun on a winter's day – they walk the streets of the neighbourhood, talking to all and sundry. Many of the offspring married other Chinese people, some married people of Aboriginal heritage, some married white Australians, and some married immigrants from other countries such as Italy and Greece. They all know about Cai and are proud of what he did and achieved – they are proud to have his blood and genes within them.

Out of the original sixty odd men who travelled to Australia on the horrendous ship with Cai, about two-thirds returned to China after they had made reasonable money. Many were lonely in Australia, without their culture or their woman, or Chinese children running around.

On his tombstone, above his grave, Cai asked for the inscription, originally by the ancient Chinese philosopher, Zhang Zai, from where he derived so much direction:

> Heaven is my father and earth, and I, a small child find myself placed intimately between them.
> What fills the universe I regard as my body, what directs the universe I regard as my nature.
> All people are my brothers and sisters, all things are my companions.

The End

The above story is my story. It is just a story, but I wanted to give you an idea of the richness of the lives of the early Chinese who came to this country. I was also inspired to write it based on all the Chinese Australians I have met and interviewed. I would like to think that Cai, and the others in the story, such as Gongshe or Fuju, are a composite of all of those people, or rather, that all the people I interviewed are an extension of them.

Indigenous Australians and Chinese Relationships

The first contact with the First Australians and the Chinese gold seekers had both in a quandary. The Aboriginals were concerned that the newcomers were neither black nor white, and so they had no frame of reference for these people from which to understand them. In turn, the Chinese were fearful of the indigenous Australians and kept their distance.

Over time, the fear on both sides diminished and relationships were sought after. For instance, there were times the Aboriginals informed the Chinese that a raging bush fire was heading their way – and when the Chinese were worried about bush fires they asked the Aboriginals for direction and help. In both instances, the Aboriginals showed the Chinese how to make a fire break.

The Chinese were intrigued and interested in learning about the bush plants, the herbs and the ecological knowledge of the Aboriginals. Often times, the Aboriginals preferred the company of the Chinese.

Apparently, it was Quong Tart (referred to above), who first referred to the Aboriginals as the 'original owners' of the land.

Delegation by Indigenous Australians to China

11 April 2016: NITV, an Australian TV channel reported the first ever delegation by Indigenous Australians to China. When asked what took them there, they replied that they wanted to forge relations… it was for solidarity of Indigenous Australians, and as activists we wanted to show solidarity between all minority groups. But our main purpose was to ask the Chinese government to help us form an international lobby to put pressure on the Australian Government into recognizing us. The trip therefore, was particularly embarrassing for the Australian Government. Cheryl Buchanan, a university student at the time, told NITV's *Awaken* program that she recalled their wonderful reception in China, "They laid that red carpet out for us, they said, 'Welcome home,' so there was a sense of commonality. I ran for those gates and I beat them all – I said I want to be the first Aboriginal in China' (but I am sure there had been other Indigenous Australians who had travelled to China).

The delegation had been invited by the PRC government who funded the group's tour of China. They meet officials of the government as well as remote groups such as those in Inner Mongolia. It was these minority groups that they particularly wanted to meet with to see how they could help Australian First Nations people from their experience.

At the time, The News of Canberra stated that the group felt that they were being treated as humans for the first time. 'At home we are treated like animals…it also makes us realise what a racist country Australia is.'

The delegation showed a documentary reflecting violent clashes between an Indigenous group and the police earlier in the year in Canberra. It had made the news in China at the time. The group highlighted the perpetual abuse and ill-treatment of Indigenous peoples in Australia.

'We wanted to embarrass the Australian Government – that was the whole purpose of going there.'

The book, *The Circus in Australia* (1842-1921) compiled by Mark St Leon reported on two Chinese acrobats (Chin Foo Lam Boo), and Aboriginal performers Mongo Mongo and Harry Cardella who performed circus acts together. This was around 1861.

Gold had also been discovered in **Queensland** near Rockhampton in 1858. Approximately 20,000 Chinese worked the area. Not only was the work hard but the miners also had to contend with aggressive Aboriginals who were unhappy about the loss of their ancestral lands. Once the gold ran out, some of the Chinese went back home whilst others worked on farms in Queensland and especially in the new banana industry.

Education

A few weeks ago (mid 2018) on many news bulletins, there was much discussion of the newly released report on the Australian national university averages and the fact that the average Chinese student did better than the national average, meaning, better than the average Australian student.

I am not an academic and this book is not academic, however I do have thoughts on this. The scope of the research seemed to limit itself to just understanding the end result; that is, that the Chinese average (in Australia) was better than the national average. The reporting did not state if the Chinese students had a greater IQ that the Aussie kids. I doubt that. It could be that the Chinese kids simply worked harder. Perhaps their will to succeed is stronger and they have greater determination. We simply do not know.

It seems logical to say that irrespective of the reason, higher IQs or harder work, or a combination of both, that when these students remain in Australia and work in Australia, that clearly they are likely to pull up national averages in all areas. Having people of possibly higher IQs and with a determination to succeed must be a good thing for Australia in the immediate future and for the longer term. We often talk about a brain drain but what about a brain influx?

I have had a theory for some time, that there are almost as many Chinese students at university in China and other parts of the world as there are people in Australia. Imagine that. Every year there are more Chinese university graduates emerging than there are people in Australia's largest state, NSW. Imagine the intelligence and knowledge that is coming out of that country in numbers that simply swamp population rates of Australia?

It is possible that there are more Chinese PhD students than university graduates in this country. The knowledge, the information and the ability to grow that knowledge and information is staggering for this country of a mere 24.5 million.

Below, in the interviews, Yang, one of the girls I interviewed wants to return to Australia to do a PhD. I would think that one of her main reasons is because of competition. In Australia, PhDs are not all that common, but in China there are over 15,000 new PhDs a year and this is growing quickly. For the cream to rise to the top in China, it must be difficult.

It is estimated that almost every Chinese family in Australia has at least one member who has attended university.

Many people believe that Chinese attendance in Australian universities is a softer way to get into Australia as an immigrant. The Australian Government denies this.

From the Australian China Council website

The China-Australia Chamber of Commerce in partnership with the Australia-China Council, and the ANZ Bank offer the unique opportunity for Australian students to work in China. The AustCham China Scholarship Program provides a comprehensive career development platform designed to foster the next generation of Sino-Australian business leaders.

Reasons for high academic achievement are varied. Research into Chinese children in the United States showed that the children often modelled their parents' conscientiousness and concern for good work performance, children were goaded to success by parental demands and high expectation, and Chinese parents compared the achievement of their children with that of their relatives' children (Sue, Zane and Lim 1984). Consequently, Chinese children felt the pressure to perform well in order to give their families 'good name', and usually felt worthless or rebellious when they failed to bring honour to their families.

The above is from aifs.gov.au/

Above I said we do not know if the Chinese average is higher because of a higher average IQ or because Chinese students work harder because of that competition I spoke of in the last paragraph. It is known that there is a level of fluctuation of IQ in any individual, that it can be marginally increased or decreased as a result of how one applies the mind, and the attention to study and learning. Well, I propose that the Chinese kids start off no smarter than Australian kids, but through application they "flex" to that slightly higher level. That coupled with the competitive streak could make all the difference.

Irrespective of the reason for the higher than average results, for Australia to compete we must have an educational dominance. It is imperative therefore that we keep importing this knowledge and expertise to Australia. Otherwise, we could lag behind.

For instance, when a Chinese graduate works for an Australian IT company, chemical company, investment company, etc., then it is likely that that they will help raise the intellectual property (IP) component of that company and bring in a greater desire to succeed, just as they do in the Australian university system. Make no mistake, Australian students are also very smart and they will extend themselves to the higher performing Chinese students. The same will happen in commerce.

It may not always be that the Chinese students work harder and have seemingly higher IQs, but they do now, and it is the now that is shaping the future of Australia. It will play a significant part in economic growth, scientific progress, and social development of Australia by large scale talent and a desire to succeed.

Michelle, who I interviewed (see below), had the following thoughts on the above, which she emailed to me.

As we talked yesterday, I think **Chinese families pay more attention to education on average than Australian families,** *and that's one of the reasons why the Chinese student's averages are better than national average. Chinese people are generally more introverted, quiet. We are always encouraged to study more when our parents see us with free time. We also are more serious when it comes to studying, and improving ourselves is so important to us while I think Australians are more social.*

Also for Australian students, being local, it's easy to make friends, and so they are more social. They are also encouraged by their parents to do some sports, less study.

*In my opinion, **Australians students should have the Chinese attitude towards study, whilst Chinese, should learn Australian's attitude towards sports and socialisation**. I have seen on the news that four Asian guys in the US team won the Math Olympic gold medal. It is very interesting to see that the most successful Math students are Asian in the US. However, we hardly see Chinese in cricket, football or those sports that require very strong bodies. So, there are pros and cons of both cultures. Chinese people need to learn to build a better body and character in Australian society, while Australians should learn how to apply their talent to make a better living, although the welfare in this country will support you.*

INTERVIEWS

The following are interviews with Chinese-Australians I conducted. They are from all walks of life.

In each case, the interviewee was given a copy of the interview once I had transcribed it for their confirmation, and shown that I represented them fairly, that I said things that were correct. Where there would have been duplication of ideas across several interviews, I have left them out, so some are shorter than others. The interviews were conducted either via email, face to face and there is one SKYPE interview and one telephone conversation.

I have represented their manner of speech, as it was written or said. I felt it is more authentic they way.

The speeches are not given in any order of importance.

Ben, gave me his offering on the phone, so I did not get to meet him. It was not a long call, perhaps five minutes. I guess his age to be about thirty-five. I had difficulty understanding him because his English could have been better and he spoke very fast. He has two children, a boy and a girl. His wife is also Chinese.

Why did you come to Australia? **I first came as a student, and fell in love with Australia and the more relaxed lifestyle. But I also saw opportunities. After studying I went back to China and worked for a few years whilst I got my Australian papers in order. I have now been here for seven years**.

How do you think China is doing economically? **I am proud of China and the economic miracle that it has had. Some say that in a few year's time China will be the biggest economy.**

So, is big good? **Not on its own, but because of the raising of the standard of living there it is good… I am happy for that**.

So would you go back there to live? **I will always return, but only for holidays, not to live. There are too many people there, too much traffic, too much pollution. I will go back every few years and take my children… I want them to grow up knowing about their people… of their ancestry. Australia, is our home, and we like it very much. China is our culture, and we love that as well. Do you understand… is that possible?**

Of course. One can live in a country they enjoy, whilst connecting to their past – after all, it is our past that makes us who we are. **Exactly**.

What work do you do? **I am importing goods from China**.

Is that what you studied? **I studied engineering... mechanical, but a friend, also Chinese, asked me to go into business with him, ... it was exciting**.

You seem young, have a business, a family, so what is the most important thing to you? **You just said it... my family. Money is good, but family is more important. In China our culture revolves around family... Our past family, and the one we have today**. That is another reason why I go to China often, it is to see my parents, and brothers.

***

Wei Wei Qian

Not all are so easy (From the Chinese Museum in Melbourne)

When Wei Wei came to study in Australia it was with great sacrifice as she had to leave her two-year-old daughter and husband back in China. She was very lonely for them. But after a time she fell in love with the beauty of Australia and applied to stay. After gaining her qualifications of Traditional Chinese Medicine, she was accepted into Australia as a skilled migrant. With those qualifications she was able to bring her husband and her daughter to Australia. Sadly, her husband missed China, and could not settle in Australia and so returned to China. In the words of Wei Wei, 'Although I regretted this divorce, it was the price I paid for living in Australia. However, my daughter is here, now grown up, and is studying politics and law at University.

Wei Wei has her own medical practice where she offers Traditional Chinese Medicine, including acupuncture.

Lu Bai

A clean cut, good-looking young man, with a modern haircut, slim, glasses, and a ready smile. This twenty-eight year old came from China to Australia in 2009 to study to be a teacher and now has a Master's Degree, and three Bachelor of Arts degrees.

We had a lovely chat sitting at a sidewalk restaurant, sipping red wine late one Friday afternoon – people were starting their weekend and were in fun mode. It was warm and congenial.

He told me that of all the Asian people he most admired. **It was the Vietnamese; they probably had the hardest time prior to coming to Australia. Most came with no education and certainly no money. He admired them because as a community they protect and supported their own better than some of the other Asian communities.**

He felt that the Chinese-Australian community often did not do this. He does have Chinese friends but limits them to those who he really likes. Wanting to be cosmopolitan, he has friends from many parts of the world, including Australians.

We spoke a lot about his teaching and his love for it. His subjects are: Business Management, History, Chinese language and Accounting. Regarding the history, he has not specialised in any particular area and is required to teach history from different periods and geographical locations – but it seemed to me that he liked this because it gives him the flexibility to learn widely on the subject. One area that he mentioned that he found fascinating was The White Australian policy, which I spoke about earlier in the book.

He spoke about his students in the classroom, and I could see the love and enthusiasm he had to help these lively young people to do the best that they can. It was inspiring. However, the poor man usually only goes to bed at about 2 AM in the morning and is up at 6 AM. These long days are a result of a workload that is just far too heavy. Apparently, when one is overly proficient in the teaching world then they get overloaded with more work. The same applies in business – those who are really good get loaded with more than those who are not as good, as managers seek to get the most out of them.

When I asked Lu how long is he likely to be under this heavy regime, he said **it would be for the rest of the year. Thereafter, because of the good results his students are likely to achieve, he will be able to dictate the terms of his next position.**

As you read above, you read how Chinese students do so well in Australia. Lu's views on this: **It's because Chinese students are more motivated to do well, plus the pressure from their parents, and to honour their parents. All equals better results. For instance, in his class there are some Chinese students, who often ask for more homework. Sometimes they don't do that extra homework but most of the time they do.**

He has not been trained to teach Chinese, but yet, it is a subject that he teaches. Even though his results have been good it is one thing speaking it, and another to teach it.

It was interesting speaking to Lu about his Chinese heritage. He was very clear on how much he loves Australia, and being an Australian, even though, as you will read just now, it has not been easy.

I want to be regarded as both Chinese and Australian. Previously, a professor of English offered to improve my English pronunciation. I chose not to do this as I want to retain my Chinese accent in this English-speaking country, to be identified as Chinese, with all my ancestry.

I must add, his English is very good, with a wide vocabulary, but it is with a distinct Chinese accent.

He continued: **the school I work at that it is in a wealthy and established area, and therefore the parents are most demanding, of both the children and the teachers. This puts pressure on everyone.**

In Australia, he does not eat at Chinese restaurants because they just spoil the food. He enjoys Chinese food, but it must be "real" Chinese food, providing it is not too spicy.

We spoke of the Chinese New Year and the celebrations.

I love this time of the year. Two years ago, my parents came out from China to celebrate with me. This year was sad because all my Chinese friends had either gone back to China for the celebrations or to other parts of the world so I had to celebrate on my own. Not wanting to be on my own, I visited Australian friends. Normally on that day I choose not to speak English, only Chinese, I was forced to speak English. Also on Chinese New Year Day, I prefer to only eat Chinese food, but because I was with my Australian friends, it was only western food. This was most unsatisfactory and made me sad. Most Westerners do not understand how important the Chinese New Year is to Chinese people, and so they can never offer the right or deepest sincerity about it.

When talking about Australia, and what his impressions are, he said:

Australia is a good place, but it can be hard – you have to be a strong character to grow and survive. It does give you opportunities but xenophobia often gets in the way. For instance, some years ago I applied for twenty-four teaching posts and failed all of them for two main reasons; the first was because

I was a new graduate without experience. The second reason was because I'm Chinese – yet, there were other new graduates who were English-speaking who got the job in front of me.

I like this country very much, he said, **but I think Melbourne is too small, only 5 million people (20% of Beijing's population). As I have been to every reasonable restaurant, café, and place of entertainment that there is – I am too bored. There are not enough people here. I love the way that it is culturally diverse, people from all over the world, however it does create a lot of conflict and racialism.** ... **I was told to, "Fuck off" you China man, go back from where you come from...**

When I asked him how he handled this, I could see the hurt in his eyes and feel the shaking of his voice, but clearly, he gets on with it and does the best that he can.

In those early times when it happened, I would walk away, and try to escape the situation. But now that I have been here for a while, I have earned the right for my place here and the contribution I have made. Now I tell them back to fuck off.

But I still see hurt in him. He went on to relate a story about a young Chinese girl who had been equally abused, and the poor young thing was devastated. This also hurt Lu. But a source of comfort is the fact that it is illegal to do racist acts in Australia (it still happens though), and so with the law on his side, plus his friends as backup, he feels more positive about it.

'I am proud of my Chinese heritage so why should I back down to them?' He also made the comment that the rural areas are worse than the cities.

Earlier on I gave you Li Cunxin, as in *Mao's Last Dancer*. Lu was critical of Cunxin, saying that he represented his ballet training in an overly harsh light. I believe that almost any dancer in those days, from any country, would have worked hard to comply with the riggers of the training. He opened the topic of marrying an Australian to stay in the country, and said that at one time I saw a young Chinese girl in her early twenties with an Australian man of about forty.

This makes me feel sick at the stomach... they either have no morals or break their morals too easily.

This conversation came about because he felt that Cunxin married his first wife, a young American girl, for that same reason – to obtain a green card to stay in America.

The *Argus*, 16 May 1862 (referring to a suicide)
On Tuesday evening the deceased went to bed, and the next morning, as they did not see him, they instituted a search which resulted in finding him suspended...he having placed a branch of a tree and thus hanged himself with a line attached to the branch.

(Underneath), a piece of paper was found with Chinese script, which on being translated was as follows;

The reign of Hum Fong, 12 year, 3rd moon, 11th day. All men take note – I, Sue Kung, got disease, and cannot get cured, after spending six or seven pounds. I am very sorry for it.

After consideration, thinking that it is destiny for a man to be rich and noble, or poor and low in this world, I therefore have devoured opium (and) depart from this life. If I suffer pain once, I will escape from all future sorrow.

My little accounts is in my little box. All my relations and friends must not be painful for me. May all men who happen to have a look at this get the blessing of Heaven and plenty gold. May my brothers and mates go home and tell my parents and wife, so that they will forget me. May the authorities, after seeing this, will not put blame on my friends. I am walking a wrong step, and can't step back, just as a basin of water, having poured it over a horse's head, you cannot get back the same quantity. This is my statement (signed) Sue Kung.

How sad for this man, and his family, to be in a foreign land without loved ones, and with a seemingly incurable disease (which could have been opium addiction), it must have difficult for him. The promise of his return with his love and hopefully gold and money to help with the prosperity of his village had been dashed. The toil and hard work of the life back in China, now coupled with the sadness of a son and husband dead would have been very cruel.

Walking in Melbourne we came across a Gucci shop. There must have been a special on because there was a queue of about 100 people all lined up from within the store, going halfway down the block, all waiting patiently, well perhaps not too patiently. Upon looking at the people, although it was in Melbourne, they were all Asian, and most of them appeared to be Chinese. It shows you that people from Asia value high-quality products and are prepared to spend big to attain them, and spend time in long queues.

I do not think I have ever owned a Gucci product and could not care less.

Lu reads a book a week, all of them English, and most of them novels as a way of de-stressing from the long hours of work.

We finished our interview saying that we would like to keep in touch and be friends.

Anonymous

Anonymous (via email from a questioner) is a male in the 40 to 45 age bracket. His profession is in Data Science. He asked that his name not be revealed.

When did you arrive in Australia? **Mid 2013**

Do you like it here? **Yes**.

Why? **More natural life. People don't normally compare each other like in China**.

Do you have children? **Yes, a boy**.

Do you regard yourself as Australian or Chinese (perhaps both)? **Since I came from New Zealand first, I regard myself as 40% Chinese, 25% Australia and 35% New Zealander** (I thought these set ratios of his interesting).

Where do you regard your home to be, Australia or China? **Australia.**

Why? **My wife and son like more in Australia and they won't consider going back to China for living but I'm neutral**.

What do you love about your Chinese heritage? **Humble and industrious. Fluent in Chinese and can understand the deep part of Chinese culture.**

What aspects of your Chinese culture do you want to retain? **Humble and hard-working**

What Chinese history do you like the most? **The Three Kingdoms dynasty.**

Why? **Many stories about the period. And there are many outstanding thinkers, strategists, and militarists in this period. There is a lot to learn from them, like Zhuge liang... is a representative of wisdom in Chinese history.**

How often do you return to China to visit family friends? **Once a year.**

Are you excited to go there? **If my Mum is not living there, I will not visit China that often. It is a mixture of excitement and anxiousness. Other than visiting family, it is more stressful as most of friends in China are wealthier and friends are always keen to know what you are doing and how much you earn, etc. In a lot of conversations, since I'm living in Australia, they would like to know what kind of business we can do together. However, if I don't have friends in China, I indeed will like China more.**

What do you miss about China? **The memory of childhood and some food. Also the memory of University time with best friends.**

What is good about China now? **Fast growing, urbanization has gradually changed the many small cities into a modern cities... and meanwhile changed the people's behaviours. Now they become more polite, and environment protection awareness, etc. The change can be more noticed in the young generations.**

Are you proud of China's growth and development? **Yes, I am.**

Do you feel welcome in Australia? **Yes.**

Are you financially better off in Australia than China? **To me, not really. But I feel less stressful**.

What do you like about Australia? **Weather and living by yourself with no pressure from others.**

What do you not like about Australia? **I indeed quite like it**.

Do you have many Australian friends with whom you socialise? **I have a few**.

In Australia, what do you like or do not like about: Australian food? **OK with food.** Houses? **I like the house I'm living, other than I need to do garden by myself**. I laughed when I read that. Schools? **The schools are generally good. But the selective school system makes my son or wife very stressful, in this regards it is very similar to be in China.

Do you like working here? **Yes**.

Is there anything that you would like to tell Chinese people back in China? **I can tell that my doctor degree female colleague married with a gardener husband, which in China is kind of unbelievable. I can tell the Chinese of the natural beauty of Australia.**

A massage with a difference

I was at the Sydney Chinatown market when a Chinese woman of about forty years old accosted me, as she jumped out to "claim" her customers. **Come… you need massage**. It was then that I saw her little kiosk. How much? I asked. **Fifteen dollar for fifteen minute**. Ok, let's do it.

Later she said, **Call me Xi** as she kneaded and stroked the kinks and stresses out of my back. **That is my last name but you can call me Xi. It is the same name as the Chinese Ruler Xi Jinping.**

What do you think of Xi Jinping? **He a very good man… he help China. So is his wife, she good lady, she in music and culture.**

I did not want the massage to end as she was telling me so many things.

Xi Jinping first wife, she also good lady, but she want live in Britain, but Xi Jinping wanted to stay in China and help people… yes… very good man.

Later she asks, **Where you visit in China?**

I told her the various places and when I told her I had been to the home of Confucius in Qufu. She told me **there is a man here in Sydney, immigrated here, who is the 67th generation from Confucius… when he die, his body taken back and he is buried in the Kong Family Cemetery.**

I told her that I also have been there and seen all of the graves. For those readers who have not visited, it is over many acres and is park-like with lots of greenery and many trees. It is also a World Heritage site.

Where did you learn massage? **In China, before I come to Australia... that twenty-five year ago.** Have you been back? **Yes, was there last year**. So you have been doing massage for twenty-five years? **Yes... very hard. I do five day a week, must rest other day. Money not big, want more money but body get tired... hands get tired.**

And your husband, what does he do? **He in factory... also work hard, not much money.**

Would you go back to China? **No, stay here, very good here... But, China also good now... good for China people**. Do you have many Australian friends? **No Australian friends... all my friends from China**. I thought that this was sad to spend twenty-five years here and not have Australian friends.

A minute later she announced, **I give you head massage... You need head massage... you must have head massage... head not good.** What do you mean my head is not good?

Call me Xi, she said

You see, I explained to her, I have played this game with Chinese masseurs before. There was one in Pingyao. Ten minutes after the massage started, she said **O oh ... big problem with head... must massage head, only twenty yuan.** No thanks. **Sure... head bad must do head...** No thanks, my head is just fine. **Ok, no problem.**

A few minutes later, **Oh no, bad skin... very bad skin.** What now? **Your skin bad, need aromatherapy oil rub. I fix you, give you aromatherapy rub... very nice... little yuan, only twenty yuan.** No thank you, my skin is good as it is.

But five minutes later when massaging my feet, **O oh... big problem feet. Must do nails... only fifteen yuan... you like it.** No thanks. **Nails too bad... must do... I do nicely... you can't have nail like this.** Ahhh, I said to her as I played the game with her... my feet are best in the world. At this she giggled, so did all the other girls in the massage room.

Xi also giggled.

We parted company the best of friends. She wished me well with the book.

***

Dan Chan

I spoke to Dan in a shopping centre. I was at the center's notice board putting up a notice, hoping to get Chinese-Australians to be interviewed for this book. Dan, who looked Chinese, was also putting up a notice (as a teacher of Tai Chi). He saw my notice and asked me what it was about. We had an impromptu interview, much to the amusement of the checkout girls of the supermarket who were bored packing shopping bags.

A scientist for most of his life, now at sixty-five, he is retired, and teaches Tai Chi. He laughed (in fact he laughed a lot) as he said,

Not so much for money, but for the love of it.

He has been doing Tai Chi for many years but only started teaching about three years ago. He looked fit and bubbled with vitality. He went on to say **Australians eat too much cake and junk food – they should be more natural.**

Dan left China when he was three years old with his parents (even so, he still had a strong Chinese accent). He has lived in Canada, America, Britain, New Zealand, and for the last eleven years Australia.

When I asked him what he likes about Australia... **The open spaces**.

And what don't you like? **Oh, that's a difficult one ... perhaps Australian's dependence on America is not good. Especially now that they have that "asshole" President Trump**. We both laughed at that. He continued... **then, racialism, it's not pretty... I have been lucky, maybe because of my position as a scientist. But many of my country people have been racially abused. Most Australians are nice people but... I guess like in many countries, there is a small percentage that make a big noise. It's sad for the Muslims, as they take most of the abuse, but our people still get abuse every so often.**

Do you miss China? **No, but I left when I was very young. I have been back several time but more as a tourist**. Then he was pensive, and stumbled a bit when he said... **It would be nice to be a bit more in the Chinese culture... it is much stronger than the culture in Australia. Australia is more mixed and so the culture is diluted... where Chinese live in their culture... that's a big thing.**

He asked me why I was writing this book. When I said that it is for enjoyment, and also because my Chinese contacts feel that this book will be of interest to Chinese people in China, he was quiet for a moment, then said, **Yes... I see that... That Chinese people will like to read it**.

Our chat lasted much longer than the interview, because when I told him I also do and occasionally teach Qi Gong, it opened much discussion.

If I come back to this town, I will look Dan up, as he was an interesting man.

Jun Hao Hu

(this interview was recorded live). Jun Hao Hi arrived some fifteen years ago with his parents (from Shanghai) and works in a medical laboratory as a freelance consultant). He is fifty-four and returns to China at least once a year.

Why did you settle in Australia? **Well, it was not me that chose Australia, it was my parents. And I think they chose Australia because it has one of the best education systems in the world. They first came for a visit and loved the physical environment. I also know that for my parents, lifestyle is an important issue. And, for me, that the quality of the air is beautiful here.**

Chinese people are different, very different, but really they are the same. They have hopes and aspirations for their children, they want to make

---

Clothing

In the days of the gold rush, the Chinese immigrants wore their traditional clothes, after all, their traditional cloths were all that they knew, and it was a way to retain their cultural links back to the "homeland". For instance, in the 1850s the men wore jackets with high collars and loose trousers, and in the cities; jackets with long robes. The women wore long loose jackets with wide sleeves over pleated skirts. Most Han woman had their feet bound – the men wore their hair, as required by law, in the Manchu style with a shaved forehead, and along single plait (tail).

Over the next hundred years or so, the traditions relaxed, whereby their traditional clothing started to phase into a more Western style. These days, the only time traditional clothing is worn is at the time of celebration or a festival.

a quality life, to be educated, be healthy, have compassion for their neighbour, and to contribute for the benefit of all. And no doubt, that Australia has benefited from that. They are a good tribe to have within this country.

They also have many friends who have great wealth and they feel that there are opportunities here in Australia. There was a report in the newspaper recently that said that more Chinese millionaires are coming to Australia than any other country. And even though Australia is expensive, houses and land is cheaper than in the major cities of China. Most of these wealthy Chinese people have strong business connections in China. My dad does, and he's always going back to China.

When I asked the question, is there anything else you would like to add, he went on to say **that it is unfortunate but many Chinese tourists cause car accidents here.**

What else would you like to add? **Well, China is trying to be serious with clean energy development, and many of its companies look for opportunities to improve in this area – in fact, they are becoming world leaders. They are heavily into renewable energy, trying to be energy efficiency... they do have a long way to go to reduce their use of coal. We are now the largest users of solar PV in the world, and are leaders in this technology** (he said this with obvious pride). **We are also growing our wind power capacity, both in Australia and overseas, and even in Australia, we have the Stockyard Hill Wind Farm project in Victoria, which is likely to be the largest wind farm in Australia**.

I asked him what he liked and then disliked about his job as a lab technician. I can't remember much of what he said at first, because what followed amazed me. **What I don't like is some of the genetic manipulation.**

Such as? He took a minute to form his thoughts. **People with disabilities also add great value. We need them... ... But** (he struggled a bit with getting out what he wanted to get out) **... I am not gay but all the gay people also offer value, the dwarfs,... and those that have Down syndrome, Neuromuscular Diseases... people with phobias, and so many more. They all add to life. They are all tribes within tribes... So what I don't like is the genetic management to see many of those tribes 'lost'... a kind of "health cleansing"... or "perfection genocide". It aims to make all without imperfections, to be all the same... How boring...**

I asked him that, surely it is the people who want all this to happen, that it is the demand from the populous that push for this cleansing, this eradication, and so the big companies find the money to fund the research to pay people in the labs to do their work. Is that not the cause?

Yes, he replied, **exactly... that is the problem...**

Although not a direct interview, I found it on the following blog (**https://www.togetherweroam.com.au/open-you-eyes-chinese-is-australia-racist/#comment-60430**)

I asked permission to use it, however, I never received a reply. It is about racism in Australia towards Asian people, by white Australians, but also by Chinese people. I thank her for writing such a clear and powerful piece.

Rene wrote...

I am a banana. Someone white inside and yellow outside. This is a mildly pejorative slur used by the Chinese for someone of Asian descent that has been white washed. I take no offense in it as it describes who I am. I'm a product of assimilation; an Australian born Chinese that has shunned her heritage to fit into Australian society.

Assimilate

As a child growing up in the 80's, I had no other choice but to blend in or be ready to be ridiculed and ostracized for being different. I made cheese and vegemite sandwiches for school and tossed out the BBQ pork buns. I told my Aussies friends that I wasn't up to much on the weekend when our family was preparing a feast to celebrate Chinese New Year; the biggest event in the Chinese Calendar.

Our sinks would be filled with live seafood, tables scattered with exotic candied fruit and sticky moon cakes. The fridges were stocked with pork, ducks, chickens and containers of dried unusual foods rehydrating like slippery fungus and pungent dried oysters. There would be incense burning, red lanterns hanging, and throughout the house red diamond-shaped Chinese "good fortune" characters were traditionally hung upside down.

Our extended family would eat until their bellies were full. Sounds of Chinese crackers filled the air with celebration as kids were gifted with red envelopes filled with cold hard cash. My siblings and cousins received intricately crafted metal wire and multicoloured cellophane lanterns. We would run around the backyard with dragons and lotus flowers glimmering in the night. However, this joy was not shared amongst my mostly white friends as it wasn't a typical Aussie experience or one that they could relate to.

I tried sharing traditions with my friends. At one time, my dad almost set the house on fire when burning Chinese offerings on the anniversary of my Grandfather's death. It was meant to be funny, that the joss paper ingots we were burning for our dead Grandpa in the underworld caught wind and set a patch of lawn on fire, but it turned into something unusual and shameful, met with perplexed looks on friends faces. "That's just weird", mocked a friend.

I wish I could better explain that the custom was in remembrance of a man deeply admired and missed by my parents. I wanted to tell my friends the happiness in my dad's eyes as he laughed and painted an imaginary picture of our Grandpa shouting his mates Yum Cha in the afterlife, flooded with gold, silver, clothes and money which we express delivered through our makeshift backyard incinerator. I later realised I would blend better by leaving the Chinese culture at home, drawing as little attention to my background as possible.

Ching Chong and so on...

Sometimes fitting in is not easy and I'm unexpectedly reminded that I stand out. A group of Caucasian teenagers once surrounded my father and I as we were walking down a deserted mall in Western Sydney. "Hey Chinaman, you have money, give us your money!" My dad smiled and with his palms held out replied "Sorry."

As we continued walking, I buried my head into the side of my dad's body, wrapping my 7-year-old arms around his skinny leg. He put a protective arm around me and we marched on as they closed in. "You no speak Engrish, gimme money Chink!" Snarled a teen. There were more words I had never heard before like Nip, Ching Chong, Gook, Slanty all mixed in with profanities. Then came the pushing and shoving and we couldn't break free. My dad pulled out his wallet and offered the balance of his meagre salary, leaving us alone.

Growing up in a small country town in Victoria, with a population of 6000 and my family being the only Asian's in the town further cemented my identification with a white Australian society.

I remember the first day we arrived into Stawell (about 300 kilometers from Melbourne), my parents insisted on photos to proudly record the day we started our new family business. As if blending in wasn't hard enough, we decided to run the local Chinese restaurant. My folks might as well have tattooed Chinese on my forehead. On that day, they obliviously clicked away as my brother and I awkwardly stood there with the jeers from a few older kids and the support of their parents in the distance. There they took it in turns to make slanty-eyed faces and hiss "Open your eyes!"

F#CK OFF! we're full

Along the way I've picked up coping mechanisms to deal with the harsh reality that Australia is not as multicultural and open as the tourism board wants visitors to think. There is an underlying level of resentment that surfaces every now and again. In 2005 the Sydney race riots made international headlines and revealed the shocking level of intolerance in Australia.

There are more subtle plays of racism in Australia. There's a certain casual open racism that's inherent in Aussie culture, digs at the dirty Wog referring to the Mediterranean immigrants who arrived after the abolishment of the White Australia Policy. There are jokes at Indians that are Fresh of the Boat (FOB's) or the bad Asian driver stereotype, all masked as Aussies having a laugh. Having travelled extensively abroad, I have found that the thinly veiled racist humour is uniquely Australian.

In my home state of Queensland, I occasionally come across rednecks in cars with "F#CK Off We're Full" stickers proudly displayed. It wasn't long ago that Queenslander Pauline Hanson was voted into Parliament, made famous for her far right anti-multicultural views unashamedly stating, "I believe we are in danger of being swamped by Asians..." When I asked a Sri Lankan taxi driver how we are doing as a society about tolerance, he responded back that "Australians as a whole are not racist, but that doesn't stop me from being racially abused each week."

I never know when I will be verbally abused because of the way I look. On a sun-drenched day in the multicultural city of Brisbane, I was returning to my office when I passed a man on the busy street, he spat at my feet, and with hatred in his eyes, shouted "F#ck off back to your country!" I stopped, but the coward kept on walking. The strangers that were within earshot glanced the other way. Who is he to make me feel like I don't belong in my own beloved country?

Why are my eyes funny looking?

"Why are my eyes funny looking?" My six-year-old son asked casually one evening as he pushed his cheekbones up making his eyes look smaller. I immediately jumped to the conclusion that someone had made fun of him at school. "Who said that?" and "Why are you asking?" I should have approached the conversation in a different way, but the feeling of embarrassment and hurt rapidly overcame me. "Nobody mum, I think my eyes look funny."

I haven't been proactive in sharing my children's culture. I haven't felt the need to explain to them that they are half-Chinese, such that they haven't realised that they are anything but white themselves. My assimilated self is to blame, still hiding from my Chinese origin.

"Your eyes are like mine, and I'm Chinese" I hoped my son didn't notice the forced smile and awkwardness in my reply.

"You're Chinese!?" he proclaimed in shock. I've never claimed to be Chinese in my entire life and it felt strange to do so. As I wrestled with the statement, I came to the realisation that I am both Chinese and Australian. "Isn't it great!? You are half Chinese and half of what makes up dad, which is English, Scottish, and German". He stood up and looked in the mirror trying to work out which limb belonged to which country.

"You have family that was once from all these countries, but what you see in the mirror is an Australian boy, just like Mummy and Daddy who were born in Australia."

I hoped my son noticed the pride in my voice.

There's hope of belonging

The Chinese also have another term called "Jook-Sing" a metaphor for bamboo pole. A bamboo has compartmentalised sections; water poured from the top of the pole will not flow out from the bottom and vice versa. This means that people who are Jook-Sing do not belong to any culture.

I worry that my kids will never be accepted in either Chinese or Aussie society, caught in limbo between two cultures, and a struggle to find their identity. There is hope; Australia has a new found focus on multiculturalism, where people no longer have to adopt white Australian culture entirely to feel a sense of belonging. Rather, different cultures, customs, and race including all that makes Australia wonderful and unique is embraced and celebrated.

Is Australia racist? Build resilient kids and look for hope in multiculturalism

I'm witnessing school lunch boxes packed with sushi rolls, curries, dumplings, salads, and pasta. Calendars are filled with cultural days, and kids are encouraged to show their friends what's special about their heritage. It's a mind blowing concept as it was only in the late 70's that my older siblings were placed in a segregated classroom for minorities with English as their second language (they spoke just fine).

My eyes are wide open, if Australia is waking up to cultural diversity it's about time I make a conscious effort to show my kids just how wonderful both sides of their heritage really is.

Michelle

Michelle and I chatted in a café against the backdrop of water and boats of Hobart's (Tasmania) beautiful Derwent River. Being mid-summer the atmosphere was relaxed and holiday-like. If it was six months later, people would be hurrying with wind jackets and scarves wrapped around face and neck. Michelle, clear-thinking and with a good grasp of issues that suggested that she was older than she is. Because of this, she was easy to talk to on a deep level. She is at University of Tasmania (UTas), on a partial scholarship, studying accounting. She comes from Shanghai and has been in Australia for eighteen months.

Why accounting? **My parents are both accountants, and I like the thought of being in an office. I started a marketing degree but switched as I did not like it much, and I think accounting gives more job scope.**

You are on a study visa, do you like Australia? **Yes, very much...When I finish studying, I want to get a two year work visa and work in a company to get experience. I will then apply for a full visa.**

Is it easy to get an accounting job in Australia when you get your degree? **It is very hard. And because it is hard many companies want you to work for them as an intern for no money**

Even though you have a degree? **Yes, for one or two years for nothing!**

We spoke of many things, but later returned to the subject of wanting to remain in Australia.

You know there are some foreign people who would try to find an Australian man or woman to love, or pretend to love, and marry him or her to force a full visa. Would you do that? Michelle looked horrified, eyes and mouth open in shock. **I could never do that... No I could not do that... I will get enough points so I get in properly**.

Like the other people I interviewed, Michelle misses Chinese food, but said she has never liked hot chilli food, so she does not miss that.

Do you make your own meals? **Yes, I cook simple food every night. But one time I tried to cook**

> **A**ccording to China's Ministry of Education, more and more Australian students are studying in China. They find it is cheaper there. Additionally, student exchange programs between the two countries is also on the rise.

dumplings... I love them... ... like my mother makes them. They were terrible, so I wrote my mum and asked her. She said she would show me next time we are together... ... I also have sent a list of foods that my mother must cook for me when I go home to visit... it's a long list...

Is the food in Australian Chinese restaurants authentic? She was most animated with her reply. **They are not at all. You can see from the menu that they make Chinese food that is not really Chinese food... food that I have never seen in China. One time I went to a Chinese restaurant with an Australian man. He said this is a top Chinese restaurant. After the meal he said, that was very nice Chinese food – I thought that was not Chinese food!**

Are there Australian foods you do not like? **I do not like Vegemite** (famous Australian sandwich spread) **... but your people love it** (she said this referring to most Australians).

I asked her to tell me of myths or inaccuracies that people in China have about Australia, and Australians.

People from China are afraid to speak English when they come here because they think Australians will laugh at them. This does not happen. They listen nicely and try to understand us. That is understandable. I am afraid to speak my few Mandarin words when I am over there.

From this, the conversation deepened and she said, **in China people think that they are not as well educated as people from the West... I'm not sure if I am saying this properly... but they don't think they are as good as Westerners with things and feel embarrassed.**

You mean that they don't feel as well educated, or as worldly and sophisticated? **Yes, all. They think they lack something... something that Westerners have, and what this does is make them want to be like Westerners... to copy them... it is wrong. For instance, when I was very little, my teacher gave me the name Linda. She gave all the children English names. I think she did this so we would impress ourselves... but it does not impress anyone.**

You have the name Michelle, how come? **Well, if I was going to have an English name I must have one that I like. I like Michelle. It is stupid and ridiculous for these names. It is trying to be an internationalist... is that a word in English?**

Go on, it's OK.

And some companies give their people English names. Some of those names are childish. It is all because we Chinese do not think China is good enough.

I went on to tell her about one of the Chinese girls who I spoke to and that she feels bad because she does not have a university education. **So why does she just not go and do it** (said the clear thinking Michelle)**? In China if you do not have proper education, you don't get a proper job. Simple. She must study. But it is different here in Australia, many people don't have proper education and they still get work. Some start their own business. Not like China… hardly anyone starts a business… they all work for other people.**

After we spoke about Chinese girls marrying an Australian man to stay in the country, she asked, **what do Australian people think of mixed relationships? Do they think they are OK?**

I went on to say that fifty years ago a lot of people were unhappy about them. Especially people of strong Christian faith. You have to understand that Australia has become the most cosmopolitan country in the world. That we have, based on our population numbers, the highest percentage of immigration in the world. We have literally every race here in this country. And because of that we are used to seeing people of all colour, and that you can't stop a white from loving a yellow, or a yellow loving a black, or a black loving a white. So yes, there are many mixed marriages. In fact, a high ratio of marriages are mixed. Personally, I think this is good, I like seeing a yellow with a white, and look at their mixed child… beautiful. So we are used to this and think nothing of it.

And what about sex before marriage? Is this good. Is this what happens in Australia?

It does. It's rare that when two people in Australia get married that they are virgins. People want to make sure they are "totally" compatible with the person they are marrying.

In China, it is not so much like this. Many are virgin when they get married. But in the big cities, now there are some that "play around". But not in the rural areas. Do you think it is good to play around before marriage?

I do. I could not think of not being a virgin before marriage. I think sex, if managed properly, is good. You must love or like the partner, and the same with them loving and liking you. And mostly that is the case. Of course, there is quick one-time sex but most people learn that this is not really what they want. I went on to tell her that when I was a young man, many, many years ago, that the culture told us that we were not men until we had a girl. So I felt embarrassed until I did. At fourteen I did not feel like a man, nor at fifteen, sixteen, seventeen! It was only at eighteen that it happened. The next morning however, I did not feel any different. Yes, it was nice. The thing is, an Australian man can't be "broken in" without telling his mates... after all, I guess I would only feel a man, when other men knew of my conquest. So I had to tell my mates, and as many mates as possible... it is like going to Mars and not telling anyone, what's the fun in that? So we "boy-men" brag about it, make ourselves feel six meters tall... it's terrible what we do to try and build ourselves up. When at that age, we did not know any better... and peer pressure is a bad thing.

I know many of the young city men of my country are the same. They hunt for it, and then tell everyone... boasting... That is not nice...

Mary and Tony

Mary and Tony are two young Chinese people, about twenty-six years of age, on a working holiday in Australia. They worked mostly on farms, picking cherries and other fruit when ripe. We said hello in a car park and started chatting. When I asked the girl her name, she was loud and cheerful, as young people should be. She said **Mary**. I asked her surname, she said, **Lamb... you know, Mary had a little lamb**.

So we laughed. I then asked him his name, he was quieter and a bit shy... **Tony**.

Tony what?

Thinking quickly he burst out, **Tony... Tony has a Pony... my English surname is now Pony.**

More laughing. They were in a hurry and so I did not get to ask my questions. They were kind enough to take my information and said they would put it on the internet for all their friends, and they did because several people contacted me.

A few days later Mary phoned me and suggested we meet in a local park as the weather was nice. We did, and with kids and young mothers running around, blue sky, it was nice. We sat at a table facing each other.

After chatting for a few minutes, we got into the interview. Turns out she is thirty, but just looks younger. She has only been in Australia for three months and is allowed to stay for two years. At the end of the time she is likely to go back to Hong Kong where she will probably try and start a small business, something that she likes doing. We chatted about this for a while to try and make what she wanted to do clearer for her.

At the moment, she is not picking fruit but working in a fish farm factory that breeds salmon and then cuts them up for packaging where the fish is sold all over the world, and probably to China.

Do you like the job? **Yes, but it is not a job that I would want to do forever.** She told me that the people are nice and very fair, they treat her and the other people well. **Every shift I do something different. It is not a proper job, I am casual, we are all casual, that means that if they have no work they tell us to go home and try tomorrow. So far, I have good work time there**.

Do you prefer this work or the farming work? **This work is better. The farming work gets my nails dirty... I don't like dirty nails. Takes me too long to clean them**.

I laughed at this, thinking that I would prefer good healthy farm dirt under my nails than fish!

Have you had any problems at work? **No... ...Yes, yes, I forget that I gave me my name Mary so Australians can say my name, but sometimes I forget I am Mary, and the boss or people come and say, what is wrong with you Mary, we called you three times!!**

> **The Colombo Plan** is an initiative to help strengthen ties with Asia – the main median is aid. Australia has donated millions of dollars in assistance, with a large emphasis on the education of Asian students in Australia, of whom many were Chinese.
>
> Even though the students had to leave Australia once their studies were finished, a large number were able to migrate back once they applied for citizenship.

You have not been here for long. Have you met Australians that you can call friends? Are Australians easy to get to meet? **I have met you. You are my friend... aren't you?**

After I smiled and said yes, she continued. **No Australian friends... they are hard to meet. I can't just go up to them. I have good friends here but they are all foreigners, that like me, have come to work here. They are very nice and help me. I live in a share house** (a big house with rooms that people rent) **and so it is nice. Mostly people from the factory, and mostly Asian. The owner is Asian**.

I thought it is sad that Mary comes to this land and lives in a bubble of people from other lands, and not with Australians. I did say to her that if she stayed longer, then I am sure she would make friends with Australians.

What do you do for fun, when you are not working? **I surf. I love surfing, and started back home before I came.**

Did you have lessons for surfing? **Yes, Mr. YouTube is my coach.** We laughed about that. **I love this place, and this beach because the waves are small, and I need "small" for now.**

Have you had any racial issues? **Most people are friendly, but sometimes I can tell someone does not like Asians or me.**

***

Joe

Joe (wants his privacy respected, so we will call him Joe) is thirty-six years old who has been in Australia for three years. A pleasant looking man, smooth skinned, short hair and bespectacled. Tall, with an easy and intelligent way about him – a thinker.

I chatted to him at his place of work, which is an aged care facility in Tasmania. Joe came from the Fujian Province in China (which is the reciprocating state/province of Tasmania). When he came, it was with his wife and parents but he now has an eleven-month-old son, who he is very proud.

Joe had trained as an electrical engineer in China, but when arriving in Australia he felt that that vocation would not suit his lifestyle with his young family because it is likely that he would have to relocate his family and live in remote areas. Joe made the decision to change his job and studied to become a nurse, and now is on the way studying to become a registered nurse. Although he did not say it, clearly he is very gentle and supportive to the elderly in the facility, as I was able to witness the way he interacted with them – it was good to see.

When I asked him what he likes about Australia he said, **the freedom of movement, the air quality, and that Tasmania, in fact all of Australia, is a paradise…. I also like the multi-culturalism of Australia, and that it is good that there are so many people from all over the world settling here, which according to him, is like polyculture (robust) as opposed to monoculture (fragile) in sustainable farming.**

There are aspects that he doesn't like here **but these things are not unique and are also fairly common to many countries of the world – so one might as well just get on with living.** He did say **that he felt** that some immigrants seem not to appreciate this country and what it offers… that they should at least be mentally prepared before they arrive. He said that the bureaucracy in Australia, especially in the public sector, as being reported by the media, surprised him and that he was not expecting it over here. **Some teenagers are being spoiled by the law for the misconduct that they commit. And the punishment for certain crimes is probably not harsh enough because the current punishments appear to be an insufficient deterrent. It is wonderful that there is excellent welfare, but financial supports should be allocated to those who are truly in need as there were reports about welfare abuse and fraud… and that the taxpayers are unfairly paying for that laziness and inefficiency. I also think that more Australian should be involved in the environment protection as it is closely related to the welfare and overall wellbeing of the current and future generations.**

When I asked him what he misses about China, he was very quick to say **the food. I miss the food from China**, and he told me about the hot pot! (I have had the hot pot in China and loved it).

I asked him if he felt that the Chinese government would be unhappy about people leaving China to come to Australia to live. He said that the Chinese government has no restrictions on people leaving the country, and that they probably realise that there are benefits to China for people to go to different countries to live. For instance, many Chinese-Australians send money back to China. Often they learn different skills and return to China to share those skills. The relationship between China and Australia is a good relationship, and to see this, now there are at least eleven cities in China that do flights directly to Australia, more so than any other country. He went on to say that he was proud of China because it has made great advances and achievements in technology and living standards over the last twenty odd years.

Ken

Ken emailed me and asked if we could use Peter Chang's story.

Ken

There was an instance I remember when my sister had her boyfriend and his dad over for dinner. There was casual discussions about Asian national pride etc. I have no attention span or interest in politics. He then asked me, hoping for an autonomous hard encoded response, "Where do you come from, my boy?" I looked up from my game boy and just said "I'm Australian." He then tried to get a different response asking, "No, but where are YOU from." My response. "Australian." Many more iterations transpired, until he realised I had no interest in giving him the answer he wanted. Twenty five years later, random people I meet still ask the same question. "Where are you from? No I mean, where do you come from. Where are you REALLY from? Your parents?" Etc. I will always frustrate the socks off of anyone trying to small talk my outwardly projected ethnicity, giving them what I believe I am, and not what they want to tell me I am.

Being an Australian Chinese means I don't have to live up to anyone else's expectations as to what it is I am meant to be. It is fantastic that as a teacher, I have many students who ask what colour my hair is naturally. I have exotic coloured stylised hair. They see past my ethnicity, seeing me as a fellow Australia and a human being.

Helen Yang

Helen Yang was kind enough to give me an email interview where she filled out my questions. She is a twenty-six year old student from China, studying in Australia, arriving in July 2015.

So what are you studying? **Master of Management (Accounting and Finance). And now I am applying for the PHD, hope that I can come back to Australia.:)**

Helen definitely likes it here and said, **lovely people, clear air, safe food, high quality citizen, Melbourne culture is wonderful (street artists, always have different activities and performance), have more time to enjoy life (less tension).**

Even though I have been to Australia for two years, I prefer eating Chinese food, making Chinese friends, and watching Chinese TV series. I just feel it is too hard to get into the culture of a new country, our culture is very different. I "know" something about Australia, I "understand" China better.

For the question, what do you love about your Chinese heritage? **I love my country, so I love all heritage it has.**

What aspects of your Chinese culture do you want to retain? **All the things I learned from very young, are all Chinese things. Maybe humility, which was from Confucius.**

What Chinese history do you like the most? **Ancient history. From kindergarten, teachers would teach about the Chinese history, lots of famous people and famous stories that can help me understand our country and love it. I go back to China once a year for our Spring festival. But, it is a good time to look at the world** (away from China), **and get know about different culture, it is a good time to widen my horizon.**

What do you miss about China?....**Taobao (online shopping, I told my mum one reason let me go back to China is Taobao☺)**

What is good about China now? **I have been travelled to some different countries, and to be honest, development of China is the fastest one. One time, I stayed at home during the weekend, and when I went out at Monday, I found there is a new footbridge near my home, which was built in two days. Last month I have been to Beijing, Beijing is much bigger than last time I visited it (two years ago), and there are more high buildings in the CBD. I am proud of China's growth.**

A comment from me, if that bridge was to be built in Australia, it would take a minimum of a month. By the time officials did a million signing offs, and builders, well... that is another story...

Do you feel welcome in Australia? **Yes, no matter, in the university or anywhere else, many convenient things can help freshmen feel better. I am a big fan of postcard sending, I change postcards**

Helen Yang

with the people all over the world, and I always say that I love Melbourne so much!

What do you not like about Australia? **High consumption** (too expensive). **Such as the public transportation, in Melbourne, if you take over two hours, it is over $7.00, I cannot remember exactly. But in Harbin, it is only $0.2 for each time, if you change another bus, you need to pay another $0.2. Most of time, one ride can take you to most places you want to go.**

Do you have many Australian friends that you socialise? **No, all my friends are Chinese**.

What do you like and not like about the food? **Starbeef, cheese and milk (also you can eat the food from many different countries (I love a Korean restaurant in Melbourne, I think it is better than the food I eat in Seoul).**

And the houses here? **Most apartments have a gym and swimming pool, fire detection and garbage classification (when I go back to China, each time when I throw away a plastic bottle, I will think that it should be thrown into to a recycle bin, but, we do not have it)**

Schools? **I only know about the university. When I have children, I will send them abroad, for them to choose the courses they like (in China, elective courses are all assigned by the school).**

Is there anything that you would like to tell Chinese people back in China? **Now, the thing I miss so much in Australia is the air – I am in Harbin, and the air condition is so bad, I miss the blue sky. I already got sick four times for five months. In Australia I did not sick for two years.**

Last time I ate hot pot with my friend, and she ask me about Australia because her brother is studying in Sydney. One of the restaurant staff heard our talk and she asked me about the food and something about the culture, if I feel comfortable there. All are about the daily life, I think most people are concern about living.

Dr Carl Chung

Dr Carl Chung (veterinarian) I packed my bag and computer (which is really my office) and headed to the country's capital, the Australian Capital Territory, specifically Canberra, where I was to look after my brother's house, but more importantly his two beloved dogs, whilst he and Kathy went gallivanting overseas for a month. It was only a day or two after they had gone that the elder of the two dogs, the male, Dunstall, developed a cough. It would not do for the dog to expire whilst I was in charge of him. Therefore, I took him to the family vet and that is where I met Dr Carl.

The doctor, as I learned later, is twenty-six years old and came to Melbourne with his parents from Taiwan in 2009. As a vet I found him to be most caring and sensitive to the needs of Dunstall and the owner (although, I challenge the word "owner" of pets, as I don't think we own them, we care for them, we love them, and in turn, they usually love us). Amazingly, in this day and age, he even took the time to phone me several times afterwards to see how Dunstall was and if the new medication made any difference. It seemed to me that this young man was giving "old time service".

After about ten days of interacting with the doctor, I explained about this book and asked him if he would consent to an interview. He was quick to say yes, but then after a thoughtful moment said, **that I may be ex-**

Australian Born Chinese in Australia refer to themselves as ABCs.

An interesting snippet
In the 1860s, about fifteen Chinese men were charged with unlawful gambling. The police came and arrested the gamblers in the midst of a game. There were about 150 men in the room, and as the police arrived, all were told to stay put, but many burst through the boards of the walls and escaped. But the men in the middle were apprehended, and one, obviously the banker, and his assistant were seen shoveling money into their bags and pockets as fast as they could.

The money had been confiscated by the police and much of it was never seen again. The banker was fined twenty pounds and the others five pounds each.

The local paper reported on the absurdity of our courtroom system of swearing in witnesses, especially the Chinese people. In the matter of the banker, who was to be prosecuted, they, the court, had great difficulty about the proper method of swearing him in. It seemed that the usual practice of swearing Chinese witnesses in is by blowing out a light. This was not considered proper, and after some discussion a representative for the Chinese man made the statement that the true method should be by cutting off the head of a fowl, which apparently displeased his Honour Judge Skinner, and the representative was summarily dismissed. In time however, the banker agreed to be sworn in on the Christian Bible, even though he knew not for what purpose it was.

There are many Chinese gambling tourists who fly into Australia, and stay in one of the city casinos and gamble for their time here. Some win, some lose.

ABC Radio National, 14th July ran a story that said that most Australian-Chinese prefer to get their international news in Chinese.

Dr Carl Chung

pressing the opinions from the point of view of my parents as they know the homeland better.

It was interesting that he used the term homeland, because when I asked him where is home, he said, **most certainly Australia**, which is fair enough. I asked him if Taiwan in any way represented home. He said **not really**, but as we continued chatting over my green tea and his hot chocolate, it became perfectly obvious that he has his Australian home, but he also has his traditional or cultural or ancestral home, which is Taiwan in China. He craves the food, and culture. Later it came out that even now, he still loves the ancient stories of his land. He also goes back regularly and enjoys his time there. Of course, he visits his grandmother there and is obviously very close to her. As she is getting older, he will keep going back as often as he can.

It seems though, that he has yet a third home, perhaps more of a spiritual home, and that is Japan. He has been there four times and can speak the language (his third language) and would like to go there and work for some time as a vet – distant future. However, he would have to study veterinary medicine all over again in Japan in order to work as a vet there.

I asked him when was it that he knew that he wanted to serve animals as his vocation. He knew exactly. It was in year three in Taiwan when he read books by James Harriet, (using the pen name of James Alfred "Alf" Wight) who was a vet and wrote about his vocation. From that, Carl had no doubt, what his calling was. It would seem that James's love and respect for animals was imbued into the ethos of the young Carl. For Carl up to that point in time had very little contact with animals, as in Taiwan there are not many, animals or pets. When his parents suggested that they would like to go to Australia, Carl was keen. He knew that Australia was a land of pet lovers and that with his aspirations of becoming a vet, he would do much better in Australia.

In 2009, the Chung family of four immigrated to Australia. His father (trained in telecommunications) quickly got a job. Carl and his brother continued their schooling and then university, whereby Carl's elder brother qualified as a teacher. His parents live in a suburb of Melbourne, which has a large Chinese community. When Carl visits his parents for holidays or quick visits, he only speaks Mandarin to them and would not consider speaking English to them at all, as that is how they have always spoken to them. Taiwan is always a term for "back home", and although he loves Australia and is grateful to Australia, he feels he is allowed to have two homes, and why not? In a lower and sad voice, he expressed his concern that in Taiwan there is a lack of respect for animals when compared to Australia, and said that the people have a lot of learning to do when it comes to animals.

Speaking about the education that he was given in Australia, he felt it was better than what he was received at the time in Taiwan. He feels that Australian students are encouraged more to think outside of the box. He thinks this gives more opportunity for creative and intelligent expression, which are handy traits for a vet. He did go on to say that he felt the education in Taiwan and mainland China has probably improved.

Whilst talking about his university studies, I asked the question, does he have an outstanding HECS loan? (A HECS loan is a loan offered by the government to subsidies university fees. Nevertheless, it is a loan that incurs an interest and must be paid off. For many graduates in Australia, paying off this loan can be a monumental effort as the amounts can be really high. There are stories of some graduates who are only likely to have theirs paid off at about the age of forty-five or fifty. Of course, this inhibits the professional from buying a house or accumulating other necessary assets.) At my question, Carl gave a self-conscious laugh, and said, 'Yes I do, and I have been in denial of its existence.' He went on to say that he fully intends to look at it very soon and start reducing the amount. He did say that his loan was not as high as other students were and that he was lucky in that respect. Once he knuckles down to it, it should not take too long to be paid off.

Carl's story as a qualified graduate is similar to those of the other interviewees who tried to find work after their first years out of university. He found it difficult with many of the companies only wanting to pay peanuts, as they said… we are giving you the experience. Carl had one such job in Melbourne but unfortunately felt it was not the right place for him. A friend, a vet study colleague, called him and said that she was working at a clinic in Canberra and they were looking for someone, and that she had told them about him. That was two years ago and Carl is very happy in that clinic. I sensed that after work hours, which tend to be long, he spends a lot of time alone and is lonely for his family in Melbourne. So it is probable that in years to come he will move back to Melbourne but only after this time of acquiring the requisite experience, and some funds behind him.

Although he has some Chinese friends, he does not actively involve himself in the Chinese community in Canberra. He also has friends who are not Chinese, but the little time available outside work he limits the number of people he gets to spend time with. On top of that, when he is not working he has housework (which he hates), washing and ironing (also yuk), and of course cooking his meals, and although he follows his mother's recipes, the food does not look or taste the same as his mother's! He went on to say that when he goes to visit his family, his mother "stocks him up" on her home cooked frozen meals for him to bring back.

As I said my farewells to this kind and caring vet, I knew that my brother's dogs were safe.

After notes of the interviews

All who allowed me to ask them questions were happy to oblige. In most instances both parties found it fun and interesting. I know I did.

What was obvious from these was that for those who have made Australia their homes, they love Australia. Equally so, they are proud of their heritage and Chinese culture. They are truly of duel citizenry. Those that have made Australia home are grateful to Australia. Most had had some uncomfortable times with racism, but recoganise that most Australians are fair-minded people. What came out of the interviews is that it is not easy to "make it" here, and that it can be difficult finding your place, but if you persist, you will make it.

When I said goodbye to each of these beautiful people, I felt that I had made another good friend.

I thank every one of you for your time and openness, and the interesting information that you gave me. Your personality is within the lines of these pages…

What will Australia look like in fifty years' time? Or is the face of Australians literally changing?

Of course, there will be the technical explosion, which is already shaping our lives. As this book is about people, not things, I do not refer to this – I am talking about people. Nor am I discussing artificial intelligence, of which there will be an abundance, nor sci-fi... nope, not virtual reality, it is real-reality, people reality... I am looking at human intelligence and human emotional intelligence, not robots. Of course, it seems that we will not be 100% biological as there will be componentry in everyone by then. Still, separating this as well, who will the people of Australia be... what will they be like? What of our societal interaction? In fifty years' time, we will find it hard to discern the difference with reality and digital reality, as digital will have enmeshed itself with the so call "normal reality".

Once again, back to people, real people, not things. People who have aspirations, people with children to raise, people who want a comfortable life, without too much stress. People who have healthy interaction with other people, because surely that is the pinnacle of life... people with other people – people sharing ideas, and cultures, sharing their emotions, people supporting other people, and of course sharing Australia.

Earlier in the book, I spoke of the voluntary component of the Australian infrastructure, that is, people helping people. It is people receiving help from people. I have also spoken much about the good as done by many of the people, such as my fictional character Cai in his story, and all Australians who have done so much to help fellow Australians, Asian-Australians, Aboriginal-Australians, African-Australians, European Australians – all of these are just plain Australian-Australians, with different skin colours, different accents, different shaped eyes, but Australians nevertheless.

So back to the question of what Australians will be like in fifty years – well as I am not a futurist, I cannot rightly say. However, I do have opinions and my strongest is that people need to remain people, helping people, enjoying people's company, not overly governing people, an equal playing field for all people, made up of the mixing-pot of the world.

Worldwide population growth is slowing, but because those living are living longer, shoulder room will be difficult to achieve. Australia is blessed with wide-open space, and if we manage this properly, there will be enough space for all, even if the projections put our population in fifty years' time at about 50 million.

However, we do need constant topping up from immigrants from all over the world. Migrants give vitality to a nation. They promote a continuance of labour in an aging population. Migrants stimulate the income through consumerism, support a higher tax revenue base and so an economic future is ensured, for without a strong economic base a country flounders, withers and is taken over by more powerful countries. It is immigration into this country that will help to secure our borders, through economic strength and strength in numbers.

Investment analysis theory say that with diversity comes better financial security. A country is the same, when it has a wide diversity of minerals and crops, then they also have a hedge against collapse – Australia has wide diversity. Not just mineral and crops, it is people diversity, and that is a great hedge.

As suggested, the current population ratios are likely to be extrapolated into the future. However, the current ratio of Chinese-Australians may diminish. The reason is the sorry plight of the rest of the world as Australia is one of the largest countries for immigration (based on per person of the existing population). It is probably one of the smallest net importers of people in relation to the number of immigrants as opposed to the size of the actual land.

However, with that sorry state of the world, Australia is likely to be called to help rescue refugees from war and poverty ravaged nations. Australia will help these people, and so they should from a humanitarian point of view. This could mean a shrinking of immigration from other countries, as Australia reaches and even exceeds its deemed annual rate of immigration. But the needed mix will be there, but not necessarily with as many coming from China. There will be more from Africa and Asia, so the visual change from pretty much a Caucasian race of people to perhaps darker-skinned, but with Eurasian features could occur – how interesting.

Who are these new immigrants? In the past, immigrants from China were poor and did manual work. Now, many are well off and come here to capitalise on what they can offer Australia. Many, have a strong infrastructure in China, and so create a two-way relationship, importing and exporting to and from, both countries. Just about all of them are well educated. These immigrants will help to cement bilateral relationships between China and Australia. To encourage this there are numerous organisations, such as The Australia China Business Council, of which we spoke above.

These immigrants bring another important aspect – they are wealthy, some very wealthy. With this wealth, and their contacts, both here in Australia, and in China, they are powerful influences. They will influence the economy and the way goods are bought and sold. In view of the fact that China is now the second largest economy in the world, Australia is likely to be a beneficiary. But the opportunities for both countries are vast... we need each other.

It is hard to believe that Australia has more land mass than the United States of America.

Australia is roughly three quarters the size of the Chinese landmass.

With immigration, there is always a balance between bringing as many immigrants as possible but not too many to swamp current infrastructure.

At the moment immigration into Australia is set at about 190,000 people per year.

Last week Australia just reached and past 25 000 000 people. It is likely that that the person who was the twenty-fifth million was Chinese as Chinese immigrants exceed births in Australia.

Currently Chinese immigrants make are the largest migrant group at 15.8%

According to Chinese-Australian artist Lindy Lee "that the alchemical "force of nature between cultures creates new cultures and new possibilities.

If, as mentioned earlier that Chinese students do raise the standard, that will play out in all aspects of commerce.

Perhaps though, Australians should not be talking about separate or disparate racial groups, or what separates us, but rather let's talk about what binds us. Whereby we remain proud of our heritage, but interdependent on each other. Every single foreigner who comes to this country brings a rich culture that is imbibed with hundreds or thousands of years behind them. A tapestry, ever weaving the Australian character and appearance.

So by now, at almost the end of this book, you may be wondering what is my heritage? Yes, I am proud to say that I am a mish-mash, a mongrel as the Aussies say. My father was Polish, French and Swiss. My mother was German. I was born in Australia. But beyond one or two generations we have not searched, however, there could be a bit of Russian in there as well. I am lily white. I am also Australian, but perhaps influenced with having lived in Africa for over thirty years, and many years and countries travelled.

Early on in the book, I gave the following: in the 2016 census, Chinese ancestry makes up 5.6% of the Australian population.

There is no doubt that the face of Australia is changing, where roughly 28% of Australians living today were not born in Australia. If we look at the number of people of two generations in Australia, that is, people born in Australia but from parents who came from other countries, the figure is close to 60%. When looking at these figures it prompts the question what is the Australian character? More important, whom will the Australian character be in fifty years' time based on what you have just read.

An analogy: get a glass of water, and put in a little white dye powder. It will change the colour. Then mix a bit of yellow, more colour change will result. Add a bit of black, and brown, and more yellow, and perhaps more white. It does not matter what the final colour will be, after all, it is only skin-deep. Let the Australia of fifty years' time embrace this diversity to mould a new Australian culture, one where the expansiveness of the land influences us for expansiveness of cultural makeup. One where we look back to the past 60,000 years of continuous occupation by our Indigenous First Nation's people, for without recognition and inclusion of them, we as a nation will be a poor one. It would also be a nation that if one of our cultural groups is disenfranchised, then all will be disenfranchised as well.

Remember above, Senator Bill O'Chee said that he did not like the term multiculturalism, and felt that all the cultures make this nation. If that happens, then Australia us in good hands.

Bibliography

Australian Government – Department of Trade and Foreign Affairs http://dfat.gov.au Australian Bureau of Statistics www.abs.gov.au/ausstats/abs@.nsf/lookup/3412.0Media%20Release12015-16both National Archives of Australia From The Global Game Changer by Doris and John Neisbitt *Sydney Morning Herald,* especially 27 July 1903 (death), 1 August 1903 (funeral), 29 August 1903 (Elite Rooms contents sale advert), 5 May 1908 (property sale advert), 27 April 1917 (Maggie's death). *Daily Telegraph*, 27 July 1903 Chris Pratten (ed) (1999). *Summer Hill*, ADHS. Ashfield Council Bicentenary history files (c. 1986–88), compiled by Linda Avramides. *The Advertiser,* 1889 (Canterbury mission), 19 April 1890 (the Mongolian), 1895/6 Mrs Tart (1911). *The Life of Quong Tart: or, how a foreigner succeeded in a British Community*, WMMcClarety, Sydney.

Manning Clark (1981). *A History of Australia*. V, MUP.

Manning Clark (1986). *A Short History of Australia*. Penguin, revised edition.

The Illustrated Sydney News, 29 November 1888, 22 April 1893.

Myra Willard (1923). *History of the White Australia Policy to 1920*. MUP.

Brian J Madden & Lesley Muir (1988), *Campsie's Past.*

Lindsay and Roger Thwaites (undated), *History of Araluen*. Braidwood & District Historical Society.

Australian Town and Country Journal, 5 August 1903.

The Bulletin, cartoons as referenced. 'The Chinese question'

The Chinese Experience in Australia – A Brief Outline for Stages 3– 5

https://book.douban.com/review/1277827/ http://www.abc.net.au/btn/v2/australians/kee.htm
http://hillendfamilyhistory.com/history/bushrangers/sam-poo/ **https://en.wikipedia.org/wiki/**

Sam_Poo https://cv.vic.gov.au/stories/immigrants-and-emigrants/language-a-key-to-survival-cantonese-english-phrasebooks-in-australia/donald-is-my-home-george-ah-ling-c1884-1987/ https://en.wikipedia.org/wiki/List_of_Chinese_Australians **https://honours.pmc.gov.au/honours/search https://en.wikipedia.org/wiki/Shen_Jiawei https://aifs.gov.au https://www.bendigotourism.com/about-bendigo/history/bendigo-gold-rush** www.worldpopulationreview.com **www.abs.gov.au** The National Museum of Australia **https://en.wikipedia.org/wiki/First_Opium_War** http://www.mudgeehistory.com.au/contents/contents.html http://www.accca.com.au/index.php

www.ingramcontent.com/pod-product-compliance
Lightning Source LLC
Chambersburg PA
CBHW060459010526
44118CB00018B/2466